CAN CHRISTIANS LOVE TOO MUCH?

About Margaret Josephson Rinck:

Margaret Josephson Rinck was born in Bridgeport, Connecticut, and grew up in nearby Trumbull. She is the eldest of six children (five girls and one boy). Her parents are devoted Christians who reared all their children to know the Lord through their own Christian commitment and involvement in missions, which influenced Margaret to become involved in Christian vocations and ministry.

She graduated summa cum laude with a bachelor's degree in psychology from Gordon College in Wenham, Massachusetts. She received the Master of Religious Education (M.R.E.) from Gordon-Conwell Theological Seminary. Her doctoral degree in counseling (Ed.D.) was awarded at the University of Cincinnati in 1979. Dr. Rinck has been active in church discipleship and counseling ministries in various local churches. She was a staff associate in the college ministry at Park Street Congregational Church in Boston. She served as a missions consultant, a counselor, and staff associate at College Hill Presbyterian Church in Cincinnati, Ohio.

Dr. Rinck is a clinical psychologist in private practice in Cincinnati, Ohio. She works with her husband, John, who manages their psychology practice and Act Resources, a self-publishing venture. She is the author of various curriculum, books, and tape series on interpersonal relationships, marriage, codependency, emotional health, spirituality, and skills training. She is sought after as a speaker for retreats, conferences, and adult Sunday school classes. She periodically conducts therapy groups for Adult Children of Alcoholics and "Women Who Love Too Much."

CAN CHRISTIANS LOVE TOO MUCH?

Breaking the Cycle of Codependency

DR. MARGARET J. RINCK

PYRANEE
BOOKS

Zondervan Publishing House
Grand Rapids, Michigan

Pyranee Books are published by the Zondervan Publishing House
1415 Lake Drive, S.E., Grand Rapids, Michigan 49506

Library of Congress Cataloging-in-Publication Data

Rinck, Margaret Josephson.
    Can Christians love too much? : breaking the cycle of codependency
/ by Margaret Josephson Rinck.
     p. cm.
    Includes biographical references.
    ISBN 0-310-51471-1
    1. Love—Religious aspects—Christianity. 2. Co-dependence
(Psychology)—Religious aspects—Christianity. I. Title.
BV4639.R54 1989
248.4–dc20   89–37147
                                                            CIP

Printed in the United States of America

90 91 92 93 94 / PP / 10 9 8 7 6 5 4 3

This book is dedicated to
the Lord Jesus Christ and
His glory, as well as to
my dear husband, John Carl Rinck,
without whom this work
would never have been done.

CONTENTS

ACKNOWLEDGMENTS

Special thanks to these people who contributed to *Can Christians Love Too Much?*:

Nia Jones, my editor at Zondervan, who worked with me and provided courteous and efficient assistance as we passed through the many hurdles of a tight writing and publishing schedule;

Faith Bonniwell, who provided, out of love and friendship, emergency typing help when deadlines loomed near;

Gary Sweeten, Ed.D., Ron Halvorson, and Sandy Wilson, Ph.D., who read portions of the draft manuscript and graciously provided suggestions;

John Carl Rinck, my husband, who completed extensive research and editorial and design work on the manuscript—a result of a close collaborative teamwork effort between us; and most importantly,

Friends and clients, who, although unnamed, graciously agreed to let me share their thoughts, feelings, and experiences in this book.

Can Christians Love Too Much?

Grateful acknowledgment is made to the following for permission to use copyright material:

Recovery Publications
Excerpts from *The Twelve Steps—A Spiritual Journey,* © 1988.

Lay Leadership International
Excerpts from *Renewing Your Mind,* © 1984.

PREFACE

The following poem was written by one of my clients who is a recovering codependent. She wrote this poem for herself as a prayer, and shared it with me in hopes that it would help others understand how codependency feels. As you read this book, I believe that you, too, will understand what this poem means.

LIKE AN OREO

What is on the inside is not the same as the outside
The outside is hard, independent, confident,
    Strong to fend off the world
The inside is soft, vulnerable, easily damaged or hurt.
    The outside is like chocolate—everybody loves it.
The inside is lovable but it doesn't think so.
    The outside is responsible, caring, serving, looking to meet
        the needs of others.
The inside is afraid of failure, yearning to be special,
        needing to be loved.
    The outside says, "I can handle it, I don't need anyone."
The inside is dying for affection, seeking approval.
    The outside is proving I am worth something, I am
        lovable.
The inside does not love me, does not know I am worth
        something.
    Lord, please take special care of my inside first.
                                        By Me

13

1
LOVING TOO MUCH....

Recently I spoke on codependency at a church. Several days later I received a call from a woman who had attended the presentation. She called to object to my use of the phrase "women who love too much." She claimed that Christians can never "love too much" and that anyone who thought that a Christian could love too much (presumably myself) did not understand the true meaning of love.

While I believe that we were disputing a semantic difficulty, I *do* understand her concern. Love is central to the Christian's worldview. We love because God first loved us. Love is the greatest virtue, even greater than faith and hope (1 Cor. 13:13). Love for one another is the outward sign that we know God (John 13:34–35).

Yet, there is still a problem. As I see it, much of what passes for love often is not "genuine" love. I am reminded of C.S. Lewis's *The Great Divorce*. In this fantasy, the damned are able to take day trips by bus from hell to the borders of heaven. In fact, no one is under an obligation to return to hell; they only need to surrender their most precious sins in order to enter paradise. The example that I'm thinking of involves a heavenly spirit (Reginald) who had been the brother of a female ghost who has made the bus trip from hell. She is disappointed that her son Michael, who died as a child, has not come to meet her. The mother had wanted to go to heaven so that she could be with "my boy." Reginald explains that Michael wouldn't have been able to recognize her even if he had come to greet her. "You will become solid enough for Michael to perceive you when you learn to want someone else besides Michael. . . . It's only the little germ of a desire for God that we need to start the process." He continues to explain that the "Mother Love" to which she has proudly clung is actually a faint and poor reflection of genuine love. The mother protests, "Mother Love? It is the highest and holiest feeling in human nature." She further elaborates that she had "done her best" to make Michael happy, she had "given up" her whole life for her son. Reginald patiently explains, "No natural feelings are high or low, holy or unholy, in themselves. They are all holy when God's hand is on the rein. They all go bad when they are set up on their own and make themselves into false gods."[1]

What often looks like loving can actually be a means to control another's behavior. For example, what passes for self-sacrifice is often, in reality, selfishness. None of us are as altruistic as we appear to be or would like to be, even in our best moments. When "love" turns into control and is used to manage and manipulate others, then we are "loving too much." The children, spouses, relatives, and friends that we "love" in this way can easily get along with a bit less of our love.

Even when our love and affection is of a more authentic, self-sacrificing nature, it can still be a codependent excessive love. How is that possible?, you may ask. We love others "too much" when loving others causes us to chronically and severely neglect our own needs. This kind of love is out of balance. It is one thing for me to sacrifice *some* of my needs for an hour, a day, a week, or even for a lifetime. But when I neglect myself "for others" to the point that this becomes an

16

unhealthy pattern of behavior, I begin to love too much. Jesus knew when to withdraw from the multitudes that followed His ministry so that He could be alone or spend time with a few close friends. He understood that there is a necessary balance between loving others and loving oneself. Jesus gave lavishly of Himself, yet He knew when it was important to take care of Himself and to allow Himself to receive ministry from others.

Another way we "love too much" occurs when we submerge our identity in the relationship with the one we love. The woman in Lewis's parable is a case in point. Not only was her "love" not genuine love, but also she could only see her own identity in relationship to her son Michael—as his "mother." Genuine, healthy love—love which is not the "too much kind of love"—produces an increased awareness of our own personhood.

When we truly love another person, we free ourselves and the one we love to become, not less, but more. This is demonstrated by God's love for us. His love sets us free from fear and enables us to love as He first loved us. Then as we love one another through God's eyes, with His love, we free each other to be what He created us to be—image bearers of the Divine Majesty. So we derive our identity from Him, from who we are in Christ.

Paul talked about how all the members of the body of Christ are able to fit together in a complementary, harmonious whole, not by merging and fusing the individual members into an indistinguishable whole but by valuing the uniqueness of the individual parts. This uniqueness, individuality, character, and diversity in the functioning of the body of Christ is to be cherished. There is no basis here for the total abnegation of an individual's legitimate needs (I Cor. 12:12–26), yet sometimes we see this occur in Christian organizations, institutions, and interpersonal relationships. Scripture does speak of denial and self-sacrifice, make no mistake about it. However, we need to distinguish clearly

17

between true biblical servanthood and *narcissistic* codependent love, which causes us to lose our identity.

"Loving too much" love has another identifying feature. It
involves compulsion rather than choice. A person who loves
too much does so out of fear or because he "has to." When I
love you, serve you, help you, take care of you simply
because I am afraid that you will be mad at me, leave me,
abuse me, ignore me, or dislike me, then my love is not freely
chosen. I feel anxious, fearful, ill, or panicky if I am not doing
something for you. Instead of loving you or serving you, I am
actually addicted to you. What makes love genuine is the
choice: You choose to love me—no one compelled you to
love. People who healthily love others understand that they
are able to freely exercise a choice, and they understand that
it sometimes is appropriate to say no to some requests. The
compulsive Christian who "loves too much" cannot say no
even when he knows it is appropriate to do so.

On this earth, none of us will ever love perfectly. We are all
tainted with selfishness and hardly ever do anything without
a reward of some kind. The only person who ever loved
without "loving too much" or without needing selfish rewards was our Lord Jesus.

The mistake many Christians seem to make is that because
Jesus is the great model for our behavior and because it is
God's will for us to become like Christ, we forget about our
human frailty and do not guard against the subtleness of sin.
We assume that our frantic giving, helping, and loving as well
as our feverish volunteerism are all as selfless and perfect as
was our Lord's. We forget to ground our identity, self-worth,
and service on who we are in Christ, not upon the service we
perform for other people, causes, or institutions we love.
Some pastors would not know how to live if you took away all
the people they "help." Some parents would not know who
they are without their children. Some people would not feel
alive if they did not have a spouse that they could rescue or
"fix." Other people would find themselves "lost" without a

great crusade or project into which they could immerse themselves. We have a strong tendency, like our spiritual ancestors of whom the apostle Paul wrote, to worship the creature rather than the Creator (Rom. 1:25). We erroneously find our identity and self-worth in what we do, instead of in who we are. We reason with ourselves that doing is more important than being and develop what sounds like a works theology, not a life of grace. If we were *being* in balance, our *doing* would be in balance too.

This book, *Can Christians Love Too Much?*, examines the issue of "loving too much" and poses an obvious question: Can Christians love too much? Although there are many books about codependency, very few look at this topic from a Christian worldview. *Can Christians Love Too Much?* examines how Christians are uniquely affected by codependency and how they can break the cycle of codependency and restore their lives through God's healing grace.

The cases in this book are drawn from my extensive therapeutic work with codependent Christians. To the uninitiated, their stories may seem bizarre, but I assure you, they are typical. Names and identifying details have been changed to protect privacy and maintain confidentiality. A number of people have written their stories and are allowing me to quote them directly. I especially appreciate their openness.

You may, as you read this book, become uncomfortable. Many people find it quite embarrassing to discover that they act codependently, when all along they thought they were being "loving." Do not let your embarrassment get the better of you. Instead, use your energy, not to shame yourself, but to free yourself from unhealthy, codependent behavior! Remember, you are not alone.

2

CODEPENDENCY AND LOVING TOO MUCH

These two terms "codependency" and "loving too much" were probably first linked together in the mass media through Robin Norwood's book *Women Who Love Too Much*. Norwood described the women in her book who "love too much" as "codependent."[1]

HISTORY

Where did this term originate? What does it mean? Historically, the term "codependency" was first used in relationship to the treatment of alcoholics. Addiction specialists, who worked with alcoholics and their families, began to notice that each family member played a unique role in perpetuating or enabling the addiction process. As therapists began to reach out to the families of alcoholics, the focus remained on the alcoholic and how the family members related to him. Their codependency, as that relationship came to be called, was not seen as an entity of its own, but as strictly related to the alcoholic's condition.[2]

The next step, according to Schaef,[3] was the recognition that the enabler/codependent had his own pain and dysfunctional patterns of behavior. At the same time, people in the field, like Claudia Black[4] and Janet Woititz,[5] were becoming aware of the other codependents: the Adult Children of the Alcoholic.

At this point, there came a recognition that codependency was a pattern that went beyond the alcoholic family. The codependency syndrome was clearly evident in other dysfunctional families as well. Codependency was a condition or disorder of its own.

Many people began to label codependency a "disease." Because the concept of codependency emerged from the alcoholism treatment area, it is understandable why this label stuck. Alcoholism has been widely accepted as a disease, especially in recent years since more research on the genetic basis of the condition has increased our understanding of the condition. Thus, professionals in the addictions treatment field labeled codependency as a disease also. Their rationale is usually that a disease has an *onset*, a *definable course*, and a *predictable outcome*.[6] As applied to alcoholism, it is fairly easy to see how these criteria led people to conclude that alcoholism is a disease. Most people in the chemical addiction field use this same logic with codependency. (In the section on addiction we will look more closely at the disease concept and whether or not it is really a "good fit" for codependency.)

DEFINITION

In its development, codependency has gone through an evolution. At first defined only in relation to the *alcoholic* family system, it is now defined more broadly. Actually there are probably as many definitions of codependency as there are codependents! However, the best definitions focus on four main points:

(1) Codependency is a learned pattern of attitudes, feelings, and behaviors.

(2) Codependency makes every area of life painful.

(3) Codependency causes the person to lose his sense of identity, and

(4) Codependency causes people to seriously neglect their own health and well-being.

Friel & Friel have an interesting definition, which is one of the best:

> Codependency is a dysfunctional pattern of living which emerges from our family of origin as well as our culture, producing arrested identity development, and resulting in an over-reaction to things outside of us and an underreaction to things inside of us. Left untreated, it can deteriorate into an addiction.[7]

Let's look at the Friels' definition more closely. "**Codependency is a dysfunctional pattern of living ...** " The word "dysfunctional" means not-functional or something that does not work. Some patterns of living work; others do not. The idea of a pattern is important. Rockelle Learner, in her work and teaching, emphasizes that it is a pattern we *learn* and it involves *attitudes, behaviors,* and *feelings.* So if it is learned, then we can "unlearn" it!

"**. . . which emerges from our family of origin as well as our culture. . .**" We learn to be codependent at our earliest school—the home. This early learning is reinforced by our culture, especially for those raised in a Christian tradition. We are told that we are to love one another, serve one another, put others ahead of ourselves. Melody Beattie, in her book *Codependent No More*, writes:

> Be cheerful givers, we are told. Go the extra mile. Love our neighbors and we try. We try so hard. We try too hard. And then we wonder what's wrong with us because our Christian beliefs aren't working. Our lives aren't working either.
>
> Christian beliefs work just fine. Your life can work just fine. It's rescuing that doesn't work. "It's like trying to catch butterflies with a broomstick," observed a friend. . .Caring

22

about people and giving are good, desirable qualities—something we need to do—but many codependents have misinterpreted the suggestion to "give until it hurts." We continue giving long after it hurts, usually until we are doubled over with pain.[8]

When we care for infants or invalids, taking total responsibility for another individual *is* necessary. Codependent behavior is *not* taking care of infants or brain-damaged people or others who cannot care for themselves. Sacrificing our own needs for the other's in these kinds of circumstances is appropriate. Yet even this appropriate caretaking can become unbalanced if the mother or caregiver *never* takes a break, gets time alone, or has *any* freedom from responsibility. The problem arises when codependent people misinterpret legitimate biblical guidelines about giving and caring. They make caring and caretaking their identity. It becomes who they *are*. They lose themselves in it. No longer free, they are bound to the role. Thus, they feel compelled to do it "not out of choice; not out of love and obedience to God; but out of compulsion." The compulsion is fed by fear of abandonment, the love of the power that comes from being the caregiver, and by the sense of self-righteous martyrdom felt when "they don't appreciate me."

Codependents expect perfection from themselves. If others fail *them*, *they* are excused. "He's had a rough day." "She's from a broken home." "He'll do better next time." Yet, they are not so gracious to themselves. They engage in "all or nothing" thinking. "I must *always* be 'kind'." "I should *never* mind giving up my free time for her." "Good Christians are *always* patient." "Nice people never think mean thoughts."

Women, especially, are taught from early life to accept this caregiving role as uniquely their own. Thus, young girls are asked to "Go see if Dad or your brother needs another sandwich," while young boys are trained consciously or unconsciously to expect women to wait on them. One client told me of the following incident in her home. Her parents were visiting from out of town, and at the evening meal, her father asked, "Is there any bread?" The daughter immediately got up, assuming that as the hostess it was appropriate for her to get the bread (which it was). Her father immediately snapped, "*You* sit down! Your *Mother* can get it!!" Later in the evening, he turned to his son-in-law and asked, "Joe, do you want a Coke?" Joe replied, "Sure Dad." Dad turned to Mom and said, "Martha, go get Joe a Coke."

Another example came to me from a friend. When she grew up she and her mom worked feverishly to keep the house clean, cook the meals, plan the social events, purchase the Christmas gifts, wrap the gifts, host the parties, serve the food, clean up afterward, write the thank you notes, etc. Her brother never had to do any chores and like her dad, expected to be waited on. This service even went to the extent that, although perfectly capable of doing things himself, her father had her mother remove his shoes and socks every day, and when necessary, clip his toenails! Mother never questioned these demands or saw them as demeaning.

In all the major Western religions, and many non-Western ones as well, the woman's role is seen as involving a "natural" amount of suffering simply because she is female: a daughter of Eve. The idea that suffering is the way to salvation, although a distortion of biblical truth, has permeated Judeo-Christian religion. As a result, this emphasis has caused many women to assume that the nagging, inward pain they feel from always *neglecting* themselves "for others" is normal and even good. It has also reduced their chance to accept themselves and have proper self-esteem.[9] Thus, our unique Christian culture, and our Western culture in general, has contributed to the codependency pattern developing in many lives.

" . . . **producing arrested identity development. . .**" Friel & Friel see codependent people as stuck in a pre-adolescent identity stage. Underneath the cool, in-control mask, codependents are merely "wounded children," hoping against hope that they will succeed in masquerading as adults! I believe that the Friels are right. Because of this identity crisis, codependents begin looking in all the wrong places for something or someone to fill up that emptiness where their God-given identity (sense of self) should be. Gerald G. May in his chapter on spirituality in *Addiction and Grace* admirably addresses this issue in terms of our struggle to avoid finding our fulfillment and our identity in God. He states that

> . . .we naturally seek the least threatening ways of trying to satisfy our longing for God, ways that protect our sense of personal power and require the least sacrifice. . .ways of having our cake and eating it too, ways of maintaining our attachments to things and people while simultaneously trying to deepen our intimacy with God.[10]

Little children. . .masquerading as adults, yet afraid to let go of control long enough to accept the freedom God offers.

. . . **and resulting in an over-reaction to things outside of us and an underreaction to things inside of us.**" Codependents are great reactors! They react to everything, except themselves. Most of them have denied themselves so much that they do not even know what they need much less how to get it. Yet, somehow they always know just what to do to solve everyone else's problems. They can see the answer for everyone else, but are in denial that there is any need to look within. They can focus on everyone else's destructive behaviors, but remain blind to their own.

"Left untreated, it can deteriorate into addiction." For many people, codependency is an addiction. It is as if there is a continuum of codependent behaviors. On one end are all of the people who sometimes act codependently but snap out of it quickly. All of us, particularly Christians, are vulnerable to a "rescue-attack" once in a while. It's part of being human. The problem comes at the other end of the spectrum when a person finds that he cannot *not* act codependently. The

25

ability to "snap out of it" has somehow disappeared. Slowly or suddenly what started out as merely helping Mom as a small child, has become a deep compulsion that has a life of its own.

PROBLEMS WITH DEFINITIONS

One of the problems with the concept of codependency is that there is no single "agreed to" or generally accepted definition. There are at least a dozen different definitions available. Most of these are more anecdotal than scientific. Also the concept has been applied to almost everything and everybody. For example, here are a number of the definitions easily found in the literature:

. . . a specific condition characterized by a preoccupation and extreme dependency on another person emotionally, socially, sometimes physically. This dependency, nurtured over a long period of time, becomes part of a pathological condition that affects the codependent in all other relationships.[11]

Calling codependency "love addiction," Schaeffer defines it as:

. . . a reliance on someone external to the self in an attempt to get unmet needs fulfilled, avoid fear or emotional pain, solve problems, and maintain balance. The paradox is that love addiction is an attempt to gain control of our lives, and in so doing we go out of control by giving personal power to someone other than self. It is our unhealthy dependency on others. It is. . .also a form of passivity. . .[an] attempt to collude with others so they will take care of us.[12]

Robert Subby defines codependency as

. . .an emotional, psychological, and behavioral condition that develops as a result of an individual's prolonged exposure to, and practice of, a set of oppressive rules—rules which prevent the open expression of feelings as well as the direct discussion of personal and interpersonal problems.[13]

Some theorists, such as psychiatrist Timmen L. Cermak, M.D.,[14] have called for a rejection of the more broad-reaching definitions, while advancing a concept whereby codependence is seen as a legitimate psychological concept. He believes that when codependent behaviors become long-lasting and pervasive, they develop into a pattern or lifestyle of relating to self, others, and the world, thus resulting in a personality disorder.

The view I take is along these same lines. When applied with a broad brush to everyone, any concept loses its validity or meaning. Certainly not everyone has a personality disorder called codependence. However all of us at times exhibit codependent behaviors, just as all of us feel depressed once in a while, yet are not diagnosed with a depressive disorder. On one end of the continuum, then, are codependent behaviors that anyone might fall into once in a while. Moving along the continuum are various degrees of codependent behaviors. At the far right end are those individuals for whom these behaviors have become an enduring pattern of relating to the self and others. These are the individuals we would call "addicted" to codependent behaviors (see figure 1). We will examine in greater detail the concept of codependency and addiction in chapter 5.

3

CODEPENDENTS AND THEIR RELATIONSHIPS

There are a couple of ways to look at codependency in relationships. We can examine the characteristics of the people involved and/or we can examine the characteristics of their relationships.

CODEPENDENT RELATIONSHIPS

A codependent relationship is the same as an addictive relationship. Some authors use the term "love addiction" to describe codependency relationships.[1] William Lenters in his book *The Freedom We Crave: Addiction—The Human Condition* describes six guidelines that can help us decide if any experience (including a relationship) is addicting.[2] Brenda Schaeffer in her book *Is It Love or Is It Addiction?* also lists a number of characteristics of "addictive love."[3] Incorporating the ideas of these writers into my own experience with Christians, I have come up with the following tell-tale signs of an unhealthy, codependent or addictive relationship. While my purpose is to highlight the features of individual codependent human relationships, these characteristics may also be seen in groups of people such as families, churches,

28

FIGURE 1: THE RINCK CODEPENDENCY CONTINUUM

Codependent Behaviors ⬆ ⬆ ⬆ ⬆ ⬆ ⬆ ⬆ ⬆ ⬆ Codependent Lifestyle

CATEGORY I	CATEGORY II	CATEGORY III	CATEGORY IV
Few Codependent Behaviors	Some Codependent Behaviors	Frequent Codependent Behaviors	Compulsive Codependent Behaviors
These are people who are basically healthy but do act codependently on occasion. They are able to live a balanced life style. They are able to give and receive appropriately. They are able to balance time for others and time for self-care.	These are often people who are new in a recovery program or who are mildly codependent. They are people who have learned to act codependently and who find themselves doing so often, despite negative consequences. Yet, they are aware of the problem and are able to move back into a balanced lifestyle.	These people are likely to enter or relapse into a codependent lifestyle. They neglect their own well-being. These people habitually act codependently in one or two areas of their life. They may or may not be aware of this trait. They tend to live an unbalanced lifestyle. They are prone to giving excessively (usually not on a choice basis) more than they receive. They may need help to shift to a more balanced lifestyle.	These people are addicted to acting out a consistently codependent lifestyle. They are often unaware of their own feelings and needs. For these individuals, codependent actions have become so habitual that they form a pervasive pattern of living. This pattern influences the person's entire style of living. They may or may not be aware of their compulsive behavior. They are unable to extricate themselves from this lifestyle without professional assistance.

small groups, mission agencies, para-church organizations, and others.

An experience or relationship is codependent or addictive (the far right hand end of the spectrum in figure 1) when it has the following characteristics:

(1) It is consuming. The experience wipes out or dulls the person's awareness. He feels utterly consumed by the relationship/experience. "I can't live without you" is the sentiment expressed. There is an imbalance in the relationship based on a compulsive need for each other. When this balance is threatened, intense anxiety develops and the potential for emotional and/or physical violence increases. I like to say that it is a relationship "with two ticks and no dog!" These are couples who can't live with each other but can't live without each other either! Even when the relationship is abusive, the obsession with it, the consuming nature of it remains. For example: Mary is obsessed with pleasing Saul even though he has been blatantly unfaithful to her for five years. She believes if she prays for him long enough her "submissive," nice behavior will win his "love."

(2) It provides immediate gratification: it is predictable. Each person knows at least unconsciously what he will "get" out of this relationship. Often this payoff has a sado-masochistic touch to it. For example, one partner enjoys hurting or disappointing the other, while the other partner unconsciously enjoys being hurt or being disappointed. Or one partner is the giver; the other, the receiver. Tom is a man who repeatedly dates women who taunt him sexually, but these women break off the relationship when he makes any move toward them physically. Suzanne is a woman who works a forty-hour job each week, manages the home, cares for the three children, keeps up the yard, and never expects any help from her husband Jerry. He comes home every day at 5:30, sits down with the paper, eats dinner at 6:00 with the family, watches T.V. until 9:30 or 10:00, and then falls asleep in his chair. It never occurs to him to offer Suzanne any help around the house, but he insists that she work so he can make the payments on his houseboat.

(3) **As a result of the relationship, there is a lowering of self-esteem for one or both parties and a blurring of boundaries between the two people**. Josie is a petite woman married to Sam for twenty-four years. They have three children. Sam believes that "a woman's place is in the home," and Josie has never questioned this idea, although she was offered a lucrative job in sales just prior to marriage. Although she used to have a quick wit and expressed herself on a variety of topics with a good bit of wisdom, after twenty-four years of marriage, Josie no longer says much. When they are with others and someone asks her a question, inevitably, Sam answers for her. Once when her sister pointed out this pattern to her when they were alone, Josie replied, "Oh, that's okay. Sam is so much smarter than I am. I wouldn't know what to say anyhow!"

(4) **The relationship is used to avoid pain, not to gain pleasure**. For example, Eric's wife, Marie, is an alcoholic. Eric is a passive, quiet man who was orphaned at age six, when his parents died in a train crash. Having lived in an orphanage until age eighteen, Eric values his relationship with Marie above all else, even though he long since gave up expecting her to love him. After they had been married a year, Marie became pregnant and told Eric that the child was not his, but that she expected him to raise it without question. Being a Christian, Eric did not believe in abortion, so he raised the boy despite Marie's constant taunts and remarks about his not being the "real father." Eric routinely has nightmares in which Marie leaves him or in which she lies dying in a drunken stupor after wrecking their car. He is so afraid of being alone that he maintains the relationship despite the fact that Marie continues to drink and run around with other men.

(5) **Obsession with the relationship causes the other legitimate contacts, interests, and involvements of the individual's**

31

life to be cast aside. Others are seen as a threat to the relationship or there is so much embarrassment about the partner's behavior that old friends are dropped one by one. Other times, there is such a need to "help" the other or "take care of" the partner that there is little time or energy left over to be involved with other people or outside influences.

Jeanette was an extroverted, happy young woman with a lively circle of friends. She was deeply involved at church, helping in the youth ministry. While dating Dan, she tried to draw him into her circle of friends. He resisted, but she thought it was just because he was shy. She felt sure that after they were married he'd change and take a keener interest in her friends. After the wedding, things did change, but not the way Jeanette had imagined. Instead of Dan joining *her*, she found herself joining *him* in front of the television night after night. When she suggested entertaining or going out to be with friends, he'd complain that if she "really loved" him, she'd be happy to stay home with him. When they did go out to church socials or to someone's home, Dan would sit in a corner looking sour and after an hour or so, insist that they go home. Wanting to be a submissive wife, Jeanette went home without complaint. After a while, she just stopped going to church because it was too hard to go alone and Dan made such a fuss when she asked him to go with her. Eventually, friends stopped inviting them anywhere because Dan either refused to come or acted so childishly that Jeanette was embarrassed. She just tried "to make him happy" at home but could not understand why she was so depressed.

(6) Genuine intimacy does not develop in the relationship. Instead, heavy dependency is confused with closeness; psychological games are substituted for intimacy; and fears of closeness keep the other at arms' length. Jack was raised to believe that men are to be cared for by women. Martha was raised to believe that a woman's needs do not count and that men are to be waited upon hand-and-foot. Martha comes home from a twelve-hour shift at the hospital where she is head nurse. She is tired and hungry and wants to fix sandwiches for supper. However, she thinks *No, Jack is a "meat and potatoes" man* (she defines him as one to be "cared for"). Jack comes home ten minutes later and (contrary to his usual behavior) offers to help fix the dinner (he tries to break out of his passive role of being "cared for" by Martha). She responds, *"No, dear. You've had a hard day too."* Martha discounts her own needs (plays victim). Jack is tuned back into his belief that men should be "cared for" so he ignores the "too" and goes off to read the paper in the den. Martha (jumping into the persecutor role) fusses in the kitchen, and finally sticks her head into the den saying, "Wish *I* had time to read the paper!" And so it goes! A chance to be close, to share about their life together, and to support one another is gone.

Another example: Martin and Phyllis have been married for thirty-two years. Martin is a truck driver on a local route. When he is at home, he insists that Phyllis be with him constantly. If he goes for a drive, Phyllis must come with him. When he goes to bed, Phyllis goes to bed. When he arises, she arises, even though she does not need to get up at 5:00 a.m. like he does. Each morning Phyllis takes out the cereal bowls, spoons, milk, and sugar. Once she had to go out of town to help her sister after a hysterectomy. When she returned home after forty-eight hours, Martin complained that he did not ever want her to go away again. She asked why and he replied, "Because I need to have breakfast in the morning and when you were gone, I did not get any." When questioned about this rather amazing dependency on his part, Phyllis said, "But he's so helpless in some ways. It's almost cute. He really needs me. It makes me feel loved."

(7) Much of the interaction in this type of relationship is based on a need to control the other person. The other is seen as the source of both potential joy and actual unhappiness. *"If only* Joe would stop drinking (or go to school, or change jobs, or come to church, or get baptized with the Holy Spirit. . .)

then everything would be okay." Often the need to control is denied with much vigor; instead the desire to "help" the other is espoused fervently. "I only want her to lose weight (stop working so hard, stop smoking, stop taking diet pills) for her own good! It's not healthy for her to do these things, and I get *so* worried!" As was mentioned earlier, the "giving" and "helping" and "loving" is not as altruistic as it seems. Underneath lies the "give in order to get" mentality. These are people who have not advanced in their moral development much past the "I'll scratch your back, you scratch mine" level. They believe that if they do the "right things," then they "should" get what they want, which is usually to control the other person's behavior.

(8) **The people in the relationships stop using their own resources for growth, fulfillment, serenity and, instead, look to other people to "make them feel good" or to take care of them emotionally.** They tend to talk in wistful terms, "If only we had a child. . ." "If only I had a new car. . .a new wife. . .a dog. . .a new church. . .a new boss. . ." They think that somehow just a little more effort on their part will be rewarded by the other person's caretaking them in return. "If I act loving just one more time when he's drunk, then he'll never do it again." "She wouldn't have left me if I'd done more. Now I'll never be happy." There is a sense of passivity as if they are waiting for happiness to come to them without doing anything but waiting for it. Or, it's as if they expect the "blue bird of happiness" to nest with them because they deserve it ("after all I've put up with"). These people have relationships characterized by dependency and domination. They lack the confidence to deal with life on their own and can only face it by being dependent on another human's strength or inner resources. Even the one who acts dominantly in the relationship is really dependent, because he fears that if he does not try to control the other, the other will abandon him.

(9) **These relationships often swing from dependence to**

34

anti-dependence. One minute I cannot live without you, the next I want "space" and need to "do my own thing." Either person can become burned out on being needy, dependent, or clingy and swing to the other end of the spectrum—anti-dependence. This is the "I'm a rock. I don't need anyone" side of their dependency. "I'll do my thing; you do yours. I can't be committed to this relationship right now." At this end of the continuum, they put a false value on what they think is "independence." In reality, they confuse aloneness with separateness. They develop a strong need to be "right" and believe that "love means being in charge or in control." They avoid their own inner pain by acting self-sufficient. The problem is that they are actually just little hurting children playing "grown-ups."

(10) There is a repetitious nature to the relationship; it seems to be a rehash of early life with parents and/or previous relationships. They repeat feelings such as boredom, jealousy, anxiety, emptiness, anger, fear, rejection, depression, and excitement in their new relationships. Old patterns and themes, such as: "I'll leave you before you can leave me" or "Come close—go away" begin to reappear. For example, scores of women have affirmed to me repeatedly the notion that in their male-female relationships they find the "nice guys" boring, while the drunks, the abusers, the workaholics, the sociopaths are *so* very attractive. Even when they *know* better, they still find themselves hooked into these relationships over and over again.

CODEPENDENT PEOPLE

When you read a list of characteristics of codependent people or look at a chart of codependent behaviors, you get the feeling that *everyone* is codependent! And in one sense that is correct: we all act codependently at times, just as we all have anxiety sometimes! Codependent behaviors are not all bad—many of them are just "good" behaviors gone awry!

It's not that codependents need to eliminate these behaviors so much as they need to *decrease* them. The difference between codependent people and "normal" (or as I prefer to term it, "functional") people is more a matter of degree than type of behaviors. Codependent people take things to an extreme, and these extreme behaviors become a pattern of living which affects how they perceive the world, act in their environment, and respond to others.

Thus, while all of us might engage in any of these behaviors once in awhile, doing so does not make us codependent. We do not, therefore, suffer from a personality disorder called codependence unless these behaviors become an all-consuming pattern of behavior, which influences all of life.

It is important to recognize that a person may be codependent and/or have one or more concurrent psychological conditions. For example, I had a client who was finally diagnosed as having along with codependency the following disorders: bipolar depression (sometimes called manic-depressive illness), borderline personality disorder, alcoholism, and an eating disorder. All of her compulsions and her codependency were greatly aggravated by her bipolar depression. It is crucial to realize that although labeling someone as "codependent" may be accurate, he may also have any number of other *serious* emotional disorders. Some people are too quick to say "Well, it's *just* her codependency," without sufficient medical and/or psychological evaluation of the person. That is why it is crucial that qualified professionals be involved in diagnosing this problem.

It is also important to understand that the work that has been done on codependency so far has been done with *adults*. Children and adolescents have *normal* dependency needs, which should never be confused with the unhealthy dependency of a codependent person.

Thus, when examining a list of codependent characteristics like the one that follows, it is important to guard against an overly simplified approach. Simply having *some* of these characteristics does not mean that you are codependent, but rather that you may be *acting* codependently these days. However, if there are *many* of these characteristics in your life, and they form a pattern that seems to consume you, then you need to seek qualified professional help.

Codependent people tend to be characterized by

(1) Over-responsibility. These are people who were "four going on forty." Everyone always told them how "grown-up" and "responsible" they were as children. They often felt as if they had to take care of their parent(s). As adults, they engage in over-nurturing, inappropriate parenting of other adults, enabling, rescuing, and caretaking. These behaviors are accompanied by a sense of "having to" do them—they have lost the sense of choice. They are experts at anticipating others' needs, while neglecting their own. Good at "people-pleasing," they rarely are aware of what pleases them, and if they are, feel guilty. They find it difficult to receive from others, preferring to be in control by giving.

(2) The over-use of denial and repression as defense mechanisms. While we all use these defenses everyday to some extent, codependent people use them too much. Repression occurs when someone is totally unaware or unconscious about something. They, for example, really "do not know" what they like or dislike or are totally oblivious to having done something wrong and act genuinely puzzled when someone else is angry or hurt because of their behavior.

Denial occurs when a person is subconsciously aware of something, but is basically ignoring it. For example, Mary knows deep inside that George drank too much but assumed that because she came from a "teetotaler" family she was "over-reacting." She thus denied that his drinking was a problem until he was arrested for DUI. Later she commented, "I knew he had a problem before we married, but I just didn't want to face it." Codependent people *repress* their own feelings, thoughts, needs, desires and *deny* the reality of what is actually going on around them.

(3) **A deep fear of abandonment**. These folks experienced "real" or perceived abandonment as children (more on this in chapter 4). There was usually insufficient emotional bonding with the parent(s). These people fuse quickly and deeply when they find relationships as adults, but as the normal routine of a relationship sets in and the infatuation fades, they experience the normal, less-intense relating as abandonment. Then they either cling desperately to the relationship or leave quickly so they abandon before they are abandoned.

(4) **A victim mentality**. Codependent people tend to see themselves as victims. They unconsciously seek out relationships that will confirm them as victims. In reality, they may have experienced actual abuse and victimization; consequently, they do not see themselves as competent or capable enough to get out of present abuse situations. The unconscious pay-off is self-pity and martyrdom, especially for the Christian codependent. They latch onto "the suffering savior" role with great enthusiasm.

(5) **A self-esteem based on achievement or belonging**. These people see themselves as worthy or valuable, not because of their creation in God's image but because of performance, achievement, or belonging. "If so and so loves me, then I'll be okay." "When I get my Ph.D., then Dad will approve of me and I'll get on with my life." "Someday my kids will appreciate all I've done for them."

Often, codependents had parents who conveyed the idea that "if a B was good, an A was better" and never seemed pleased or happy with the child himself. These adults now believe that "nothing is good enough" and some even contemplate suicide when they are not performing perfectly. They are overly sensitive to rejection and tend to blame themselves for anything that goes wrong in their relationships.

They link "belonging" with people-pleasing and so are

hesitant and/or unskilled at being assertive. They believe that "everyone" knows better than they do, so they settle for being needed rather than loved or appreciated. Under all their over-achievement, they feel totally unlovable and find it hard to believe or feel that even God could love them.

(6) **A tendency to develop obsessions and compulsions**. Obsessions are thoughts that become a habitual focus of attention or anxiety, while compulsions are behaviors in which they feel compelled to engage. (This point may or may not include the formal Obsessive Compulsive Disorder [OCD] diagnosis.) They are compulsive and obsessive about relationships and situations. In relationships they focus all their energy and feelings on other people; confuse pity with love; and feel compelled to "help" others "for their own good." In situations, they only feel alive when there is a problem, crisis, or tragedy. They are reactors not actors, and live as if addicted to excitement and chaos. They find serenity boring!

(7) **A tendency to focus on what "could be" rather than the reality of what is**. Codependent people are always living for "someday." "Someday Mom and Dad will accept me." "Someday Joe will realize how much I care." "He has so much potential. Someday he'll stop goofing off and give his life to Jesus." "When he finishes law school, then he'll be able to be with us. He won't have to work so hard then." "She's so sweet, sometimes I just live for the day when she is kind all the time."

Codependent people find it difficult to face reality. They latch on to "diamond in the rough" type of relationships and then try to be the catalyst that polishes the diamond. They ignore the abuse, the sinfulness, the selfishness, the indifference or meanness because "someday my prayers will be answered." Always living for tomorrow, they let today slip by unnoticed. Often, they spend their lives waiting . . . waiting for the other to love them, be nice, accept Christ, stop drinking, stop fooling around on them, and so on. All the while they ignore what the person is really like; what he or she really does; and how he or she really behaves.

One client of mine deluded herself into believing that for nineteen years she had had a "happy Christian home." All the while, however, her husband, an elder in their fundamentalist church, had beat her and the children and had compelled her to submit to sado-masochistic sexual behaviors. This woman's desire and longing for a "loving Christian family" led her to discount real physical and emotional abuse for nineteen years! To all outside onlookers, this couple did seem to be an ideal role model for Christian marriage. They had a dynamic Christian ministry and a charming family. It never occurred to the wife that she tell anyone the truth about what was really going on at home.

(8) **A need to be in control.** Codependent people have an excessive fear of loss of control. Often life as a child was so chaotic that the only way they could survive was by becoming super-responsible and super-controlling. They try to control all their thoughts, feelings, and behavior to an extreme degree. They try to control others, often by "being nice" or complying with what others want. Thus their "loving" behaviors are really manipulative. They act "loving" to gain some control over the other person's actions. "If I love him more, he'll stop working so late." "If I cook better meals, he'll come home on time." "If I lose weight, then she'll have sex with me." "If I hide his pornography, he'll read the Bible instead." "If I lay out all his clothes the night before, he won't be late for work and he won't lose his job again." As you can see, most of their controlling behaviors comes out of fear. They are usually shocked to discover that their so-called "helpfulness" to others has been a covert tool to control or head off disaster. Thus, we have seen that codependent people act in some very predictable patterns of behavior. In chapter 4, we will examine the roots which cause these patterns of codependent behavior to develop and grow.

4

THE ROOTS OF CODEPENDENCY

Underlying the codependent behavior pattern are two root problems: shame and fear of abandonment. To understand why a person acts codependently, we must have a clear understanding of these two issues.

THE SHAME EXPERIENCE

What Is Shame?

In Western culture the concept of shame is not usually separated from guilt. Often, the two words are used synonymously. Most Westerners view shame as a superficial form of social embarrassment. Guilt is viewed, however, as deeply personal.[1] Anthropologists have shown us that this view of shame and guilt is not universal. Many cultures are predominantly shame oriented. From a Christian view, Scripture actually puts more emphasis on shame than guilt. Yet, Westerners have often failed to notice this shame-orientation.

Guilt is usually seen in the West as an individualistic concept. A person becomes guilty whenever a boundary is transgressed or when there is a transgression of a specific

41

code. Guilt focuses on specific acts, behaviors, thoughts, attitudes. It's primarily a legal concept related to law-breaking. A person may or may not feel guilty in a psychological sense. Guilt is a moral concept, but shame appears to be a universal cultural concept.[2]

Shame, therefore, is a more social, less individualistic concept than guilt. It often involves a fear of criticism by oneself and one's peers. Shame in this sense seems to need an audience even if this audience is merely oneself.[3] It is a deeply personal concept as well. In her book *On Shame and the Search for Identity*, Lynd explores how shame relates to self-consciousness.[4]

Experiences in which we feel shame cause us to develop a new sense of self-awareness. We are exposed or made vulnerable to ourselves (and sometimes others) in a new fashion. Our response to a shame experience becomes either a positive self-revelation from which we grow and change; or a limiting, self-denigrating experience which we try to cover.

Thus, a person can carry deep shame over events that no one else knows about. The concept of shame involves being exposed, uncovered, stripped, laid bare. We often speak of feeling "stripped of my defenses" or react to such an experience by "covering our faces in shame."[5] Biblically, we see this need for "covering" in the beginning of humankind's journey. Adam and Eve, before God even confronted them, "realized that they were naked; so they sewed fig leaves together and made coverings for themselves" (Gen. 3:7). In their pride to have knowledge and be like God, they broke a law (standard) set up by God for them. Thus, they experienced both moral (legal) guilt and shame (a sense of dishonor, loss of self-esteem, disgrace) in their own eyes and later before God (vv. 8–9)

Adam and Eve, and hence all of us as their descendants, share a *state of shame*. Although created in God's image and hence of infinite value and worth and still loved and sought after by God, Adam and Eve became entrapped in a *state of shame*. They were exposed as fallible, frail, rebellious, proud, sinful, and finite. They had not been content with the identity God had given them: that of creatures created in His image: male and female. Instead, they sought, out of pride, to be equal to God Himself. Thus pride and search for identity led to their shame.[6]

Types of Shame

Besides being in a general *shame state*, people encounter a number of types of *shame experiences*. Each has a different flavor or nuance.[7] They are:

1. Innocent shame that occurs when someone else slanders your character or ruins your reputation. You feel shame or embarrassment because you realize others have heard this slander.

2. Guilty shame that occurs when you do something morally or ethically wrong. This type of shame is the one most Westerners think of when they think of guilt and shame synonymously.

3. Social blunder shame that involves feeling ashamed or embarrassed when you commit a *faux pas* or disgrace yourself socially.

4. Significant other shame that occurs when people are closely and unavoidably identified with the shameful behavior of another person. This type is similar to shared shame where a person participates in the embarrassing incident *with* another person and they both experience shame.

5. Physical imperfection shame that is experienced when a person is ridiculed, teased, or avoided by others due to a physical defect, or when a person feels shame over a real or imagined physical defect, even when others do not notice or ridicule the person.

6. Discrimination shame that happens when a society denigrates, downgrades, or rejects certain groups (e.g., racial, economic, ethnic, religious, social) as inferior, worthless, or evil. People in these groups may feel shame for being identified as these rejected parts of society.

7. Public punishment shame occurs when a person is deliberately exposed to ridicule, humiliation, or shame as a form of punishment (e.g., public flogging).

8. Anticipated shame that is experienced whenever you do not do something because you might be caught, punished, or exposed if you did it.

9. Modesty shame that involves some form of sexual shame. Modesty is defined differently in different cultures, but all have some standard of modesty. Even societies where nudity is the custom have some social shame associated with immodest behavior.

10. Personal-inadequacy shame that occurs when someone feels intensely inferior to others in some way, even to the extent of feeling like a nonperson.

11. Sympathy shame that often occurs when someone else experiences shame and you as an onlooker feel empathy or blush for them.

12. Compliment shame that occurs when someone blushes from pleasure or because of embarrassment that they are being noticed or given attention.

It is obvious that not all these types of shame have moral/ethical content or basis. Thus they are what I call "particular shame experiences," which may or may not be related to our shame state.

Responses to Shame

Responses to shame can vary from the momentary blush to a lifelong personality pattern. Some situations in which shame is experienced have minimal impact on personality formation; others, though seemingly trivial in themselves, are devastating for the person(s) involved and have a lifetime effect on them.

It is helpful to distinguish between being in a state of

shame and experiences of shame. All people, according to Scripture, are in a *state of shame*, due to our rebellion against God. Like our ancestors Adam and Eve, we all have sought, through pride, to find identity in things other than being God's creatures (i.e., to be our own God). We have sought to control our own destiny rather than submit to His plan for us. Thus, we are exposed to ourselves, others, and God as fallible, rebellious, proud, idolatrous, and sinful. This state of shame causes us to respond in certain ways.

In general, we respond to our state of shame by trying to hide our fallibility, our weaknesses, our problems and failures. We focus on other people and *their* behavior, seeking to transfer the shame to them.[8] Fearing that closeness and intimacy will leave us defenseless and vulnerable to exposure, we keep others at arm's length. By working too much, staying busy, using rage, control, or power plays and other defenses, we keep other people away. We develop perfectionistic habits of thinking and acting, seeking to prove that we are not shameful after all. These responses are what I call "lifestyle shame responses." This tactic is illustrated in Scripture by Cain. He sought through the work of his own hands (his garden products) to expiate his guilt and cover his shame. God pointed out to him that human works were insufficient and that only the blood of the sacrificial lamb could expiate his guilt and wipe away his state of shame (Gen. 4).

Other responses to shame go beyond the need to cover up, hide, or deny one's state of shame in general. These other responses are what I call "particular-shame responses" as opposed to "lifestyle shame responses." Particular-shame responses are those responses we have to *individual shame experiences*, while lifestyle shame responses are reactions to our *shame state*. Examples of particular-shame responses are blushing when you are caught with your zipper down; stammering when the teacher calls on you to answer and your mind goes blank; lying to your father about your grade on a

FIGURE 2

SHAME STATE VS. SHAME EXPERIENCES

A SHAME STATE LEADS TO:

PARTICULAR SHAME EXPERIENCES LEAD TO:

Lifestyle Shame Responses

Hiding our weaknesses

Blaming others

Projecting our shame on others

Defensiveness

Criticalness of self and others

Perfectionism

Works-orientation

Fear of closeness

Keeping others away or at arm's length

Power/control tactics

Compliant/overly-obedient

People-pleasing

Being "nice" all the time

Judgmental behavior

Particular Shame Responses

Blushing when your fly is down

Stammering when the teacher calls on you and your mind goes blank

Lying to your father about your grade on a test

Refusing to date after a rape experience because you feel like "damaged goods"

Changing your name to "Rose" from "Rojas" because of shame over your cultural heritage

Dressing frumpily and plainly because of embarrassment over being a woman test; refusing to date anymore after a rape experience because you feel like "damaged goods"; changing your name from "Rojas" to "Rose" because you are ashamed of your Latin heritage (see figure 2).

Obviously, a person might experience particular-shame responses even if they were no longer in a shame state. For example, people who have trusted in Jesus Christ to expiate their personal guilt and wipe away their shame are no longer in a shame state. Romans 8:1 states clearly: "There is now no condemnation for those who are in Christ Jesus. . . ." However, because of the continuing battle between what Scripture calls our "old self" and the "new self" (Gal. 5:16–26), particular-shame responses will occur. Christians still feel shame and respond with blushing when they make a social *faux pas*. Christians still experience shame in particular circumstances because they are still broken and needy and still make mistakes. Christ has transformed them from a shame state to a mercy state, but in everyday life, old shame-based behavior may remain. Old habits are difficult to break. We all know that we are "seated with Christ in the heavenlies" (Eph. 2:5–7; Col. 3:1–4), yet in day-to-day life, we do not yet experience it fully. As Paul says in 1 Corinthians 13, we "see through a glass darkly; but then face to face" (KJV). Only when we reach the heavenly homeland will we know the perfection of godliness and be free of shame in our experiences as well as in our state of being (Phil. 4:12–14; Rom. 7:14–25).

What do we say, then? Is Christ's death and resurrection meaningless in everyday life if we still experience lifestyle and particular-shame responses? Not at all. If we truly learn to understand and appropriate His work for us, which freed us from our shame *state*, we will grow in changing both old lifestyle responses and particular-shame responses. The heavenly reality will become more and more an earthly experience.

For example, before our transformation/recovery process

FIGURE 3-A: THE HUMAN CONDITION

HUMAN CONDITION PRIOR TO TRANSFORMATION/RECOVERY

SPIRITUAL	PSYCHOLOGICAL	BEHAVIORAL
Created in the image of God, of infinite worth, value; loved by God not for behavior, but because of who we are (His children), in a state of shame due to being exposed as fallible, sinful, finite creatures; are revealed to selves, others, God as less than we could, should, or want to be.	Tries to cover shame. Hides, conceals true self from others. Tries to transfer shame to others. Responds to particularized experiences of shame with defensiveness and concealment. Develops perfectionistic traits to conceal shame, seeks value and worth based on performance orientation. Fears closeness, intimacy, vulnerability because such contact might expose shame, weakness, fallibility. Develops low self-esteem because he/she allows self to feel worthless because of shame state.	Denies faults, ignores weaknesses. Becomes moralistic. Acts judgmentally. Limits self-disclosure. Keeps others at arm's length, creates a phony self. Becomes arrogant. Blames others, angry outbursts. Criticizes, holds others in contempt. Acts patronizing to others. Acts like nice person all the time. Caretaking, helping too much. Seeks to always please others to avoid shame or vulnerability. Keeps others away through working too hard, rage, prejudice, control tactics, and power plays. Acts in self-defeating compulsive ways as if to prove to others that he is as bad/worthless as he feels.

FIGURE 3-B: THE HUMAN CONDITION

HUMAN CONDITION AFTER TRANSFORMATION/RECOVERY HAS BEGUN

SPIRITUAL	PSYCHOLOGICAL	BEHAVIORAL
Created in the image of God, of infinite worth, value; loved by God not because of behavior but because of who we are: His children. Shame state removed by Christ's death and resurrection, there is now no "condemnation." Person is forgiven, cleansed, empowered to change and grow. God's mercy reaches the inner self and transforms shame state to mercy state.	Open, vulnerable, admits areas of fallibility and weakness; Welcomes critique by Holy Spirit and other people; Eager to learn more about him/herself; Does not fear self-knowledge. Responds to experiences of shame with mercy and openness to self and others. Refuses to shame self any longer because Christ has paid the penalty and covered his/her shame with His own blood. Accepts Christ's forgiveness and mercy and experiences enhanced self-esteem. Lets go of perfectionistic efforts to conceal fallibility. Recognizes value based on being created in God's image, and not on performance.	Admits faults to self and others. Examines own behavior regularly (moral inventory) not to condemn self but to confess/admit errors and be healed. Uses revelation of shame experiences to change and grow. Willingly self-discloses to others; Gives mercy to self and others rather than shaming self and others. Allows self to fail; Discards phony self and "nice" perfectionist image; More congruent, genuine, "real" in interactions with others. Does not need to use compulsive behavior or power plays to feel good about self.

©1989 Margaret J. Rinck

was begun, we had no choice but to respond to our shame state in both our lifestyle and in our particular circumstances. These responses were like those of Adam and Eve: defensive, blaming of others, critical. We covered up, lied to ourselves and others, and so on. Psychologically and behaviorally, we were reacting to our shame state. When particular-shame experiences happened, we also responded to cover up, hide, or deny the shame we felt. What difference does a personal relationship to Jesus Christ make? A big difference! Unfortunately, many true Christians never catch on to this important aspect of Christian truth. They continue to live *as if* Christ had *not* transformed them from their shame state, *nor* given them the power to break old shame-based lifestyle and particular responses.

When people give their lives to Jesus Christ and are filled with the power of the Holy Spirit daily, they will find themselves breaking those old response patterns (Gal. 5:16–23). Instead of denying their faults, covering up their weaknesses, transformed people eagerly seek to know more about themselves, and regularly take rigorous moral inventory (James 1:19–25). They know their guilt is forgiven and their shame has been washed away in the blood of Jesus (Rom. 8:1–2; Isa. 43:25; 44:21–22; 45:17; Zeph. 3:19; Rev. 21:1–4). God's mercy reaches down, and through the power of the Holy Spirit, they live no longer as children of darkness in shame, but as children of the light. Instead of responding with bitterness, defensiveness, fear, perfectionism, compulsiveness, they now respond with the fruit of the Holy Spirit (Eph. 5:1–21; Gal. 5:16–26). God's power is available to transform shame-based lifestyles and particular-shame responses into healthy, Christ-like, Spirit-produced responses. And should we fail (which we will do) and fall back into old habits, John reminds us:

> My dear children, I write this to you so that you will not sin. But if anybody does sin, we have one who speaks to the Father

in our defense—Jesus Christ, the Righteous One. He is the atoning sacrifice for our sins... (1 John 2:1–2).

Thus, transformed people are congruent. They are open and honest about their failures and can act "real" in the presence of others. No longer basing self-worth or value on works, performance, or perfectionism, they are able to let go of power plays and controlling behaviors formerly used to manipulate others and bolster their own self-esteem. No longer do they need to act judgmentally and shame others, as a way to take the focus off their own shame. Transformed people use daily particular-shame experiences as opportunities to grow in self-awareness and maturity. No longer do these experiences become occasions for self-flagellation or compulsive behavior (acting out). See figure 3 for an overview of this process.

THE ABANDONMENT EXPERIENCE

What Is Abandonment?

Most people when they read of or hear about the concept of abandonment do not believe it applies to them. They think of abandonment in extreme terms, thinking only of babies left in trash cans as "abandoned." In reality, there are many types of abandonment that can happen to a person. Some forms of abandonment, while not involving actual physical desertion, do involve neglect of basic human needs. Other forms of abandonment involve actual abuse.

Emotional Abandonment

The essence of emotional abandonment is that no one is there *for the child.* The child is left unprotected. No adult is available to meet his needs. Even when physical needs are met, a child can feel abandoned. For example, a father provides physically for the family. There is a home, car, food, and other necessities. However, he must work two jobs to

51

provide these. When he is at home, he is exhausted and has little patience for a child climbing all over him. Or, perhaps mom is unable to emotionally connect with her child because as a child herself she was molested or physically abused. She never learned how to connect safely with others or how to be affectionate. Thus, her child experiences her distance as abandonment even though she loves the child deeply. People from these types of homes experience emotional abandonment. They "know" their parents loved them, but never "felt" loved.

Neglect is not always intentional or malevolent. Sometimes it occurs because the parents are wrapped up in caring for another sick child or a sick grandparent. Sometimes the neglect is beyond anyone's control, such as when a father dies and the young mom is forced to work and thus is unavailable to her children,

Obviously, some people do experience actual desertion by a parent or parents and for them the sense of abandonment is even deeper. However, we tend to discount the pain children who were emotionally abandoned experience, forgetting that from their viewpoint, they still *felt* abandoned.

Shaming Feelings as Emotional Abandonment

Not providing for the emotional affirmation and reflection a child needs is one way emotional abandonment happens. Another way is when feelings are denied, shamed, repressed, punished, or ridiculed. God created us with the ability to feel. Feelings are neither good nor bad—they just are. It is what we *do* with the feelings that matters. Feelings were created as a type of monitoring defense to let us know what is going on. If I walk down the street and someone grabs me by the neck and my heart starts to pound, and I feel flushed and angry, it is because my "fight/flight" system has gone into action. The same thing happens when we perceive ourselves to be "under attack" emotionally. The angry feelings are like the red light on the dashboard of a car which warns us that our oil is low. Smashing the red light so we do not see it anymore does not help us deal with the problem of low oil! Yet many Christians believe if they suppress their feelings, they are "solving the problem" (i.e., the problem that created the unpleasant feelings). Thus, they shame themselves and their children for having feelings, or if not for having them, for showing or expressing them. This shaming of feelings has a devastating effect on the growing child's emotional life and self image.

Bradshaw[9] outlines the purpose of various emotions on our lives. **Sadness** involves the discharge of energy around pain and helps us heal and grieve the losses that we all experience. When sadness is denied or repressed, the pain is frozen within us. This freezing of the pain can lead to depression, despair, and even suicide.

Fear alerts us to a threat to our basic needs, physically, emotionally, spiritually, or socially. Discernment and wise action can result from listening to fear appropriately. When fear is shamed, it can become terror, phobias, or paranoia.

Guilt moves us to take action and change when we have violated our values or transgressed our standard of morality.

Joy is the emotion that signals all is well and that all our needs are being met. When joy is shamed, people learn to feel guilty for having fun.

Shame tells us that we are limited, finite, not super-human. It makes us aware of our human limitations.

Anger warns us that our boundaries have been violated. It is like the red light on the car dashboard. Anger when shamed becomes bitterness, resentment, and rage.

All emotions are gifts from God to be used wisely and not degenerated or neglected. Yet in many homes, emotions are shamed, considered foolish, improper, or childish. Some people, while not denying their feelings, shame themselves with phrases like "Oh, I shouldn't feel that way" or they shame others by saying "Oh you don't feel like that!" So we learn to hide, repress, and ignore how we feel. The feelings go underground, however, and begin to wreak havoc even though people do not realize it.

Even in the most caring homes, this form of emotional abandonment can happen. It happens because the parents, well-intentioned as they may be, were shamed for *their* feelings, and so the sins of the generations are passed from one to another.

The problem is that many parents never received proper nurturing themselves and so are incapable of passing it on to their own children. Thus, parents who were emotionally abandoned unconsciously look to their child to fill up their own need for admiration, acceptance, and identity. The child becomes the mirror for the parent rather than the other way around. Instead of the parent taking charge of the child's emotional needs, the child ends up caretaking the parent. This experience of parental reversal is a form of emotional abandonment. No one is there for the child. The parents may be sensitive and caring but unable to connect with their child due to their own emotional losses in childhood. Outwardly they encourage the child, but the child is not nurtured because the interpersonal connection is broken. The child comes to believe he is loved as a performer, not as a person. The child's true authentic self is abandoned because the parent could not connect emotionally.[10]

Results of Emotional Abandonment

What happens to a child whose need to be admired for who he *is*, not for performance, is not met? Or, for whom Mom or Dad remains a shadowy, austere, albeit benevolent, figure?

One result is a disconnection from feelings. The parent never models connection to feelings, and the child is thus never able to experience his feelings without shame. Or he may not be able to feel them at all. He becomes someone who knows how to *do* but not to *be*; to *think* but not to *feel*; to *talk* but not to *cry*.

A child in this situation also develops a "phony self." This self is not the true person inside, but rather is a creation by the child of what he perceives others expect of him. The child becomes detached from his true self and ultimately is unaware that it even exists. Unaware of his own needs and feelings, this child becomes performance-oriented, always seeking approval by *doing* and achieving.

Ironically, this type of person may develop a false sense of closeness to his parents. He comes into therapy profoundly depressed, yet sincerely believes that his childhood was wonderful and the relationship with his parents, healthy. In reality, this "closeness" he feel is enmeshment. He cannot experience himself as a person separate from his parents because he is so needy and desperate for their approval. Detached from his real self, and projecting the phony self, he lives with the illusion that "all is well and we're very close." He does not realize that he was emotionally abandoned and mistakes his enmeshment with intimacy.[11]

Abandonment Through Boundary Violation

Another type of abandonment involves boundary violation. Boundaries are the borders of oneself; the personal space each of us has around us. Boundaries are physical, emotional, psychological, and spiritual. We have all experienced boundary violation at some point or another. For example, when you go to a party and someone leans too close when talking to you, your automatic response is to back away. Your physical boundary was crossed. Most of us are aware of these physical boundaries but are less aware of emotional boundaries. In some homes, physical and emotional boundaries are inappropriately crossed, causing great damage.

Here are examples of boundary violations:

1. The father who continues to bathe his ten-year-old daughter.

2. The siblings who walk in on one another in the bathroom without knocking.

3. The mother who confides in her teenage daughter or son about her unhappy relationship with their father.

4. The pastor who regularly takes his young son with him on pastoral calls, saying to the son that "It's good to be away from Mom, isn't it?"

5. The mother who calls her married son every day to see if he ate breakfast or remembered to take his umbrella to work.

6. The parents who insist on knowing the salary of their daughter's husband.

7. The young boy who takes on the role of caretaker and responsible child, getting his siblings off to school because Dad is working and Mom's too depressed.

8. The daughter and mom who cannot make a decision without consulting one another, even though the daughter has been married twenty years.

9. The parents who decide where their child should go to college, even though the child would rather go to vocational school.

10. The mother who acts offended when her college-age son locks his bedroom or bathroom door.

11. The little girl who becomes the "homemaker" and "Daddy's girl," because Mom and Dad don't get along very well.

12. The parents who cannot understand why a twenty-nine-year-old son wants to move out and get his own place to live in.

13. A child who witnesses his parents engaging in sexual behavior, due to unlocked doors.

14. Parents walking around the house naked or allowing children older than age three or four to do so.

15. A dad who asks his twenty-one-year-old daughter if she still is a virgin or what her menstrual cramps feel like.

All of these examples illustrate types of boundary violation. In each case, some line of respect has been crossed, creating a situation where shame, fear, anger, and pain can develop. All human beings need to maintain boundaries between themselves and others. Without boundaries, a person is helpless and defenseless. Parents who model strong boundaries in their own lives help children develop strong boundaries, too. By identifying with the parents when they set a boundary, the child learns how to do so for himself.

For example, if a child consistently sees Mom set limits on Uncle Harry's rude behavior, the child learns that (1) it is okay to hold people accountable for their behavior; (2) even relatives do not have the right to act rudely or abusively; (3) women can stand up to men and protect themselves; (4) it is normal to feel strongly when someone else violates our boundaries. By watching Mom appropriately set boundaries for herself, the child develops an internal model for use in his own life in later years.

In homes where boundaries are not modeled and where they are also violated without comment, children do not develop the inner strength needed to create appropriate boundaries. Often people wonder why a woman continues to live with a man who emotionally or physically abuses her. Whenever I have encountered a woman who does not leave such a man, I have also noted that she does not know how to set up appropriate boundaries, and in fact, usually does not even know what they are!

Sexual Abuse/Neglect

One form of boundary violation needs special comment. This area is the violation of sexual boundaries. Such violation is unfortunately one that is generally ignored in the church. People are too ashamed, embarrassed, and frightened to admit that this type of abandonment/abuse has occurred to them or is occurring in their homes now. Sexual abuse happens to little boys as well as to little girls. It involves both covert and overt sexual acts. Tickling to the point of hysteria is just as much a sexual violation as actual rape. Sexual comments directed to or about a child can do just as much damage as physical groping. Boundaries are boundaries, and whether they are physically or overtly violated or covertly or emotionally violated, the damage is there. We need to face these facts and create an atmosphere where it is safe for people to begin to deal with these issues without shame.

Abandonment as Neglect of Basic Needs

All people have their basic needs: physical, mental, emotional, social, spiritual. Generally speaking, these needs are hierarchical in nature. That is, if one's physical needs are not met (lower needs in the hierarchy), then it will be difficult to focus on meeting higher needs such as social or spiritual needs.

Figure 4 outlines the basic needs all people have. In our Western way of thinking, we categorize needs and place them in hierarchies as mentioned above. There is some merit to this approach in terms of understanding and differentiating these needs from one another. There is a danger, though, in artificially separating them into categories. In real life, no one experiences his needs separately. Everyone's needs overlap or impinge on one another. For example, when I am hungry (physical), I find it difficult to concentrate (mental), become irritable (emotional), and may be critical or rude to those around me (social and spiritual). Also in the church there is a tendency to over-spiritualize needs or make spiritual needs or spiritual decisions the only factors in a person's life. Rather than being spiritually centered, many evangelicals have become spiritual reductionists, viewing things as "*just* spiritual" in nature. These people fail to understand the complexity of our creation. For example, sin manifests itself in a number of ways other than the spiritual in our human na-

FIGURE 4

BASIC HUMAN NEEDS

PHYSICAL: stimulation/touch, being held, caressed; medical care; food; warmth; shelter; clothing; water; sexual contact.

MENTAL: stimulation/excitement/challenge; pleasure; pain; play; security; peace of mind; boundaries.

SOCIAL: structure; limits; predictability; consistency, attention; being regarded as special; guidance; modeling, identification with significant others; time with significant others, feedback.

EMOTIONAL: affirmation of needs and feelings; encouragement; praise; warmth; affection; sense of self as separate from yet cared for by others; sense of uniqueness and worth, of being wanted or valued for oneself.

SPIRITUAL: grace, mercy, forgiveness; redemption, repentance, sanctification; maturity; gifts of Holy Spirit; ultimate glorification.

ture.[12] There is societal sin (e.g., apartheid); there are effects of sin across generations (e.g., alcoholism, venereal disease passed on to an infant, child abuse). Yet many Christians seek "spiritual-only" answers and neglect societal or generational systems needs. Basic needs are basic—with no single set of needs being the only "really" important needs.

When children's basic needs (as outlined in figure 4) are neglected, they begin to experience certain deficits and learn to view the world in a certain way. They learn to feel unloved, not valued, unimportant. As their needs continue to be consistently unmet, not only do they feel abandoned but these children learn to shame themselves for *having* the needs in the first place. The logic they unconsciously use goes like this:

> It must be my fault that my needs are not being met. If I mattered or had any value, my parents would meet my needs. I must be hopeless and utterly without value. I'm no good. If I were good, then they'd care for me.

It never occurs to children that something might be wrong with Mom and Dad. After all, in their minds, parents are gods. Parents can do no wrong. Ultimately the interpersonal link between the child and other humans breaks down, too. The child believes "I have no right to depend on or need anyone."[13] Thus the child feels shame for being needy and for being alone (abandoned). Either way the child blames himself. Shame heaped on shame eventually causes the child to lose all awareness of basic needs. The child develops a phony self, which is usually compulsive in some fashion. Compulsive perfectionists or compulsive sexual acting out or compulsive manipulation of other people would be examples of the type of shame-based behaviors these children develop. Figure 5 illustrates the shame-based personality development process.

FIGURE 5

SHAME-BASED
PERSONALITY DEVELOPMENT

SHAME STATE
DUE TO ORIGINAL SIN

PLUS

BASIC HUMAN NEEDS

PLUS

NEGLECT/ABUSE/ABANDONMENT

LEADS TO

UNMET BASIC NEEDS

LEADS TO

PARTICULARIZED SHAME
Child thinks: "I'm no good"; "I don't matter"; "I'm unlovable,
unlovely"; "I'm hopeless, worthless, utterly without value"; "I'm
not worth being taken care of."

LEADS TO

INTERPERSONAL LINK BETWEEN CHILD AND OTHERS
BREAKS DOWN
"I don't deserve to need anything."

LEADS TO

MORE SHAME ACCUMULATING
—shame for being needy, human
—shame for being alone, helpless

LEADS TO

LACK OF AWARENESS OF ONE'S NEEDS

CULMINATES IN

DEVELOPMENT OF PHONY SELF
USE OF COMPULSIVE BEHAVIOR AS COPING MECHANISM
TO HIDE FROM SHAME AND FEAR OF ABANDONMENT.

ATTACHMENT/BONDING/
SEPARATION/ABANDONMENT

It is far beyond the scope of this book to explain fully the concept of attachment and separation. An excellent text for those who want a more thorough approach is *The Psychology of Separation and Loss* by Jonathan Bloom-Feshbach, Sally Bloom-Feshbach.[14]

For our purposes, the concept of attachment-separation is of crucial importance with regard to the basic fear of abandonment. Early caregiving relations, chiefly with parents, provide for children a psychological foundation from which they can later form other relationships. Learning to be close (attachment/bonding) and learning to separate (differentiate) are developmental tasks all of us must achieve in order to mature. A child who does not learn to be close and how to detach from others finds it difficult as an adult to face ambiguity and aloneness. Coping with loss is a lifelong endeavor and those who do not learn how to do so early in life suffer long-lasting consequences.

From the moment of birth (and some would say even before birth) an infant's behavior becomes organized in such a way as to bring the child in closer contact with the parent or caregiver. Usually around six to seven months, an infant orients to a particular caregiver, usually the mother.[15]

Development of the *separation* response depends on the extent to which a child has made significant *attachment* to the primary caregiver. When a strong bonding to the mother has occurred, the child will manifest a variety of responses to separation. Research indicates that secure early attachment "predicts longer attention spans in children, more display of positive affect during free play, and more autonomous play activity and better use of parental help in problem solving. . ."[16] Children who are secure in their attachment to mother and other significant people find it easier to separate from them. Children who are not securely bonded to their parents find separations more traumatic and are more fearful of abandonment as children and later in life. All children develop a fear of strangers (at about six to nine months) and separation anxiety (at about six to twelve months). Children who did not enjoy secure attachment to significant others, however, find future separation more anxiety producing than children with secure attachments. Such tolerance of separation is necessary for a person to mature and develop a separate sense of self.

Bowlby and many other researchers have helped us understand the importance of this process.[17] Donald Joy in his books *Bonding* and *Re-Bonding* explains these concepts in lay terms and within a Christian context.[18] It is important to understand this attachment-separation need if we are to help the codependent person achieve healing. Obviously, people who are fearful of abandonment and who have learned to live with shame, due to early childhood experiences, will be more likely to develop unhealthy patterns of living, such as codependence. Getting to these root patterns will make healing more possible.

5

CODEPENDENCY—
AN ADDICTION

There is a tendency in evangelical Christian circles to view addiction as "just" a spiritual problem. "If they'd just find Jesus," or "If they'd just make Christ the Lord of their life," or "If they'd only be baptized in the Holy Spirit" are typical Christian cliché reactions to people with addictive problems. This individualistic, pietistic view of the human condition falls short of a true biblical perspective. It tends toward a Greek-Dualistic view, not the Judeo-Christian view. While we would all agree that the spiritual part of life is central, it is not central in the sense that it is the "only part that counts." The Judeo-Christian view of human beings is that they are a united entity—"all one piece, as it were." For the Hebrew, there was no sacred/secular split, no dualism. "Spiritual" things were not "better"; they were "merely" part of life. In a real sense, *all of life* was spiritual, not just the aspects of life that we label "spiritual" today.

In my training course *Renewing Your Mind*, I made the following observations about the Christian education program outlined therein. These observations about an educational training program are equally relevant here, whether we speak of a Christian therapeutic or remedial program.

Our beliefs matter! It is important for us to understand the basis upon which a training program like this rests for two reasons: (1) Our belief systems shape all that we do, providing a foundation for every educational activity. (2) In order to be effective, our educational programs must be based upon valid observations of what people are really like as well as sound biblical teaching.

If our presumptions or beliefs are faulty, then everything we build on that foundation will be faulty. That is the reason this course is based on a solid foundation of both biblical teaching and scientific fact.

ALL TRUTH IS GOD'S TRUTH

The reason we can have such a solid and balanced foundation is because all truth is God's truth. When we speak of truth here, we mean something which is real, active, and personal. Truth in this sense is not merely a set of beliefs, concepts, or verbalizations. It is something that has an objective reality in an open system, that is, it really exists in the universe. (An open system includes the spiritual or supernatural realm whereas a closed system includes only those things that can be detected by our five senses or with the help of scientific instruments.)

GOD REVEALS HIS TRUTH

God reveals His truth to us in two ways: through creation or nature and through His plan of redemption. Theologians have termed the first type of revelation general revelation or common grace and the second, special revelation or special grace.

We see God's revelation in creation or nature (general revelation/common grace) depicted in some of the following passages:

So God created man in his own image, in the image of God he created him; male and female he created them. (Gen. 1:27)

Here we see that God created mankind in His image to reflect who He is.

The heavens declare the glory of God; the skies proclaim the work of his hands. Day after day they pour forth speech;

night after night they display knowledge. There is no speech or language where their voice is not heard. Their voice goes out into all the earth, their words to the end of the world. In the heavens he has pitched a tent for the sun, which is like the bridegroom coming forth from His pavilion, like a champion rejoicing to run his course. It rises at one end of the heavens and makes it circuit to the other; nothing is hidden from its heat. (Ps. 19:1–6)

Here we see God revealing Himself in the heavens, His creation. God's invisible qualities (His nature) can be understood by observing His creation.

Through redemption (special revelation/special grace) we see God revealing Himself through His Son and the Scriptures, as shown by the following references:

John 1:1–5: Here we see that Jesus is the Word of God, the ultimate revelation of God to mankind.

John 14:6–11: In this passage we observe Jesus telling His disciples that He is one with the Father.

Colossians 1:15–20: Here Paul expounds the supremacy of Christ, the image of the invisible God.

Hebrews 1:1–3: The author of Hebrews reminds us here that God has spoken in the past through the prophets, but now He speaks to us through His Son, who is the exact representation of His nature.

Psalm 19:7–11; 119; 160: In these Scriptures we see the law of God or the words of God being extolled as perfect. They are the truth by which we should live.

2 Timothy 3:16–17: All Scripture is here presented as from God Himself and an appropriate guide for living.

Thus, we see that Scripture clearly affirms both general revelation (creation) and special revelation (God's Word and God's Son). Whether truth is discovered in nature or in Scripture, it is still God's truth.

GREEK DUALISM VERSUS CHRISTIANITY

Unfortunately, many Christians are unaware that they have adopted a Greek-Dualistic way of looking at life rather than a biblical worldview. They see some things as "spiritual" and, therefore "good," and other things as "unspiritual" and, therefore "bad." For example, they believe they are acting in a "spiritual" fashion when they pray, but they are not being "spiritual" when they take time out to play with their children. Or, they believe that going to church is "spiritual" but making love with their spouse is "unspiritual." They mistakenly confuse this outlook with biblical Christianity, when it is merely Greek Dualism.

Greek Dualism is a way of viewing life that divides everything into two basic categories. The term "dualism" refers to a belief that there are basically two types of things in life—good things and bad things. The Greeks believed that the material world (our bodies, human activities, physical surrounding, and so forth) was evil, while the spiritual world (nonphysical realities, mystical truths, God, heaven) was good. In their view, the less a person had to do with the evil, physical world, the more spiritual (and hence a better person) they were. Some early Christians mistook Greek Dualism as a Christian way of looking at life and incorporated it into their theology. Both the apostle Paul and the early church councils of the third and fourth centuries condemned Greek Dualism as heresy.

The true Judeo-Christian position is that life is viewed on a wholistic basis. Human beings are a unity (body, soul, spirit). There is no sacred/secular split, with some things in life being more spiritual than other things. All of life is holy because it is to be lived to the glory of God. All of life is under God's Providence, and thus no vocation or calling in life is more spiritual than another.

CHRISTIAN AND SCIENTIFIC RESEARCH

Due to their Greek-Dualistic worldview, many Christians have a limited understanding of God's revelation in creation. As was mentioned earlier, the Scriptures clearly teach that God has revealed Himself in creation (general revelation) and through His Word, both living and written. General revelation comes to our awareness through scientific investigation, while special revelation comes to us through the Incarnate Word (Jesus Christ) and the written Word (the Scriptures).

However, many Christians who are unaware that they are thinking like Greek Dualists, have fear of, or reject outright, the facts about human beings discovered by psychologists. For some reason, they have no problem accepting the authority of science when it comes to biochemistry, economics, medicine or physics. Yet, when the facts come from psychological research, they are afraid to accept them. It is almost as if they believe there is no possibility of a non-Christian scientist discovering anything true about human nature by studying the way humans behave (creation/general revelation).

The reality is, however, that since God is the author of all truth, any facts discovered by scientists about the emotional and psychological functioning of human beings are a part of God's truth, also. He is our creator. He made us function psychologically the way we do! If something is true of us as human beings, it is true because God created it that way! Thus, Christians need not fear a conflict between what God has revealed in creation (general revelation) and what He has revealed through His Son and the Scriptures (special revelation). Whether a scientist discovers facts about human nature through observation and research, or a theologian discovers them in Scripture, the facts remain equally God's truth.

The facts or observations themselves, as long as they are true, are from God. Human beings may differ, however, as to how these facts are interpreted or applied. Thus, while we need not fear the facts or data themselves, we need to be aware that a person's worldview (open or closed) may determine how he interprets the facts or the theories he develops from those facts. This is demonstrated by the existence of many different psychological theories which are, for the most part, based upon the same observations about how human beings behave.[1]

COMPONENTS OF ADDICTION

When we view addiction, we must not be tempted to look only in one direction for "causes" or "cures." No one piece of the addiction puzzle is sufficient to solve the problem. God created us as complex beings whose different components interact in a multidimensional manner. It is not easy to separate one aspect of the human condition as being *the* cause. We do acknowledge that if Adam and Eve had not sinned, illness of all types—physical and psychological problems, relational problems and societal problems would not exist. At the root of *all* human problems lies sin. *However*, it is naive and simplistic to assume that to fix all these problems "all we need is Jesus" (i.e., a spiritual experience). We all know of people who have a profound faith in Christ but still suffer from cancer, polio, cerebral palsy, depression, anxiety, or broken relationships. While a "spiritual experience" with Christ is essential to recovery from any sin-based problem, it is not the *only* thing necessary. Sometimes God uses doctors—even pagan doctors—to save the lives of Christians. Sometimes a psychotherapist or a counselor is needed to help heal a broken relationship or a wounded spirit. Sometimes rehabilitation is necessary to help the person develop a new lifestyle.

When we approach addiction, therefore, we must examine all of the components of the problem. All pieces of the puzzle must be part of the recovery process. The spiritual dimension seems to be a central or crucial piece, but it is not everything. In AA, one will often hear "Those who do not get the spiritual part of the program, do not recover." This bit of folk wisdom appears to be true. Yet, it does *not* mean that hence the "rest of the program" is not important. Prayer, while important, will not by itself keep an alcoholic sober. We humans are too complex for that.We are much like the elephant who being examined by a committee of blind people was variously described as "skinny, wobbly, firm, stout, tough, and soft." Depending on one's view, human beings look different. And so does addiction.

There are three basic pieces to the addiction puzzle. While not all the pieces have been adequately studied, we do have ample evidence to at least acknowledge their roles, while holding in abeyance any final conclusion on how these factors work together. These three components are: spiritual, psychological, and physical.

Spiritual

Spiritually, addiction can be seen at its core as idolatry. When someone is addicted to something or someone, he is placing that thing or person as central in his life. He runs his life not based on God's grace and plan for him, but based on his relationship to another person, substance, or experience. For example, the woman addicted to an alcoholic bases her life on trying to control, and hoping to cure her alcoholic husband. Similarly, a woman married to a misogynist (a man who hates women) gains her whole identity and sense of self worth on whether this man likes her, loves her, and treats her well. When he responds favorably, she is happy, content, and feels good about herself. When he does not treat her well, she is deflated, defeated, depressed.

Whenever anyone is given this amount of attention, he becomes an object of worship. The Scripture is clear: we are to have no other gods before Yahweh! Yet what one of us has not been guilty of worshiping money, or another's approval, or intellectualism, power, chemical substances, sexual gratification, children, spouse, parents, church, or theology? The list of possible idols (addictions) is endless. In one way, the root of idolatry is pride. Somehow, like our ancestors Adam and Eve, we naively believe a lie and tell ourselves that we know better than Yahweh. We succumb to the serpent's story and believe that this experience or that person will "really" make us happy *this* time. And so addiction is partly pride and idolatry.

From a spiritual perspective, we can see that addiction flows out of the state of shame in which humans find themselves. Because of their pride and need for a sense of

70

identity, humans experience shame whenever anything threatens their sense of self or their pride.[2] Prior to the Fall, Adam and Eve knew no shame. Their glory and pride was in Yahweh Himself. They knew who they were: creatures made in His glorious image. Genesis 2 tells the sad story of Satan's deception and their quickness to believe a lie. Suddenly, even before God confronted them, they were exposed, naked, vulnerable to themselves and each other. They are revealed as they were: fallible, broken, sinful. They tried to hide and cover up their shame with fig leaves. Shame thus became a universal experience. Humans experience shame as a feeling of being exposed, made vulnerable at seeing oneself as one is or as one fears he is.[3] Thus, humans are in a state of shame. They experience a loss of self-esteem when they recognize that they are less than they could, should, or want to be. Addiction, then, becomes one way of distracting oneself from this state of shame; a way of hiding from oneself and from the truth. Certainly, this aspect of addiction is best illustrated by the universal phenomenon of strong denial around the addictive behavior. Even those around the addict do not want their shame uncovered, and so the denial is maintained even to delusional proportions.

Besides idolatry and shame, addiction's spiritual components also include rebellion. Anytime people are idolatrous they are rebelling against God. Rebellion is our need to be in charge, to be in control, to manage things ourselves. For addicts, their rebellion comes out through their idolatry— their fundamental dependence on and relationship to mood-altering substances, experiences, or persons as the central focus of their life. We will look at spiritual rebellion and the codependent addict in more detail in chapter 6.

Psychological

Psychologically, addiction is multidimensional. The root experience seems to be one of shame and emotional pain. At

FIGURE 6: THE ADDICTION CYCLE

ACTING IN

A strong control orientation. Individual still feels compulsive but fights addiction. Strong fear of letting go. Must constantly be on his guard. Person shames himself because of compulsivity. Swears he won't act out again. Person tries to hold in his impulse to act out.

SHAME

A sense of unworthiness, of being "no good." Feelings of hopelessness, and lowered self-esteem.

ABANDONMENT

The fear that my shame is uncovered and that people will reject and abandon me.

SHAME AND FEAR OF ABANDONMENT

ACTING OUT

Complusions
Dieting
Working
Mental Rituals
Self-righteousness
Perfectionism
Codependency
Super-achieving
Addictions
Alcohol/Drugs
Food Disorders

Sex Addiction
Money/Gambling
Addiction to Chaos
Emotional Highs
Physical Abuse
Emotional Abuse
Sexual Abuse
Ecstactic Religiosity
Self-mutililation
Relationship Addiction
Caretaking

the center, the addict is searching for a sense of identity; a way to distract himself from pain; and a way to cover up his shame. Shame is both a spiritual state of being and a psychological experience. Psychology (and Scripture) speaks of the need humans have to cover up, hide, deny, wear masks, develop a persona, use self-concealment.

Shame is at the center of the addictive cycle of acting in and acting out (see figure 6). When acting out, the addicted person engages in his or her compulsive behavior(s).[4] Either experience (acting out or acting in) is driven by shame. When the consequences of a person's acting out become too shameful, he reverses direction and tries to control the behavior.

Unsure of their identity, the addict seeks to find it externally. Other people, the approval of significant others, work, money, power, chemicals, sexual experiences, caretaking, food, dieting, exercise, and many other experiences are used to bolster the addict's self-esteem. If the boss approves, if he earns a million dollars, if he marries so and so, if he loses weight, if he gets a Ph.D., if . . . then he will feel "good about himself." Even religiosity can be an addictive experience when the person only feels whole and secure, or only has a sense of self when he does church work, or is involved in some ecstatic experience. This search for identity and purpose is the reason some cults and mystical religions are so popular. Adherents become addicted to the self-righteousness involved; the leaders; the excitement; the sense of being unique, the chosen few, etc.

Thus psychologically we see addictive behavior as a search for identity; a need to hide, cover up, or deny one's shame state, and a way of distracting oneself from pain and emotional trauma.

Physical

Some literature describes the body's ability to manufacture chemicals that control pain and pleasure. This natural chemistry lab in our bodies could be an underlying mechanism in many "addictive" behaviors. The human body does indeed have a tendency to become "hooked" on chemicals—chemicals from the environment or from within the system itself.[5]

Sidney Cohen, M.D., in *The Chemical Brain: The Neurochemistry of Addictive Disease*[6] summarizes recent research on the neurochemistry of the brain and its relationship to addiction. It includes a discussion of genetics and addiction.

Kathleen Whalen Fitzgerald, Ph.D., in her book *Alcoholism: The Genetic Inheritance* summarizes in easily understood language the current research on alcoholism as a family disorder.[7] These are only a small sample of the fine resources available on the physical aspects of addiction.

Archibald Hart, noted author and psychology professor at Fuller Seminary, states in an article in *Christianity Today* (December 8, 1988):

> Psychological and sociological factors hitherto thought to be the primary determiners of "dependency" may well be mediated by chemical change throughout the body. The release of adrenaline in "emergencies" has long been known to be stimulating, and in recent years the discovery that the brain manufactures its own opiate-like endorphin. . .that produce a tranquilizing and pain-reducing reaction has added credence (some would say final proof) to this understanding of how certain behaviors can be addicting.[8]

The basis for a physical link in addiction and compulsive behaviors is becoming stronger. While more research must be done, it is clear that certain addictions and compulsions have a physical component. In the case of alcoholism, there is a clear genetic predisposition which sets people up for this problem. Research is beginning to link certain eating disorders to familial alcoholism. Obsessive compulsive disorder has clear physical (chemical) components. Some researchers believe that a substrata of addicted people have overlapping OCD (Obsessive Compulsive Disorder), further exacerbating their already compulsive behavior pattern. If true, this would explain why some alcoholics and sexually addicted people only get better when given certain medications (like lithium) along with their normal addictive recovery treatment. Some researchers even believe that alcoholism itself is really a subdisorder of manic-depressive illness (a disorder due to a chemical imbalance in the brain).

RESPONSIBILITY

Many Christians feel leery of any view that posits a physical basis for addictive behaviors. They assume that if a person has a physical predisposition to being addicted then he is no longer morally responsible for his actions. The church community in general has historically seen addictions as "merely" problems of lack of willpower or character. The scientific community has stressed the sense in which a person is a victim of a disease process. The reality is that both perspectives are true. The line between where a person's choice to drink, for example, is operative and where his physical dependence takes over is a fine one. No one can say "with this one action" when that line is crossed. At some point choice *is* lost, and the person does become a victim. Yet in reality, as Lenters puts it:

> In point of fact, drawing a sharp line between "victim" and "agent" is difficult and usually unnecessary. Alcohol addicts are *always* victims and *always* agents. Although they may be victimized by their addiction, they are responsible for the progression of the disorder, for the consequences of their behavior, and ultimately for getting into treatment. On the other side, although they may be agents of their own alcohol abuse and for the tragedies that lie in the wake of that abuse, they are also victimized by physiological givens . . . that precipitate loss of choice, entrapment to ethanol, and bondage to it.[9]

As evangelicals, we tend to emphasize the importance of individual decision-making. This emphasis has a proper place. We are all individually accountable to God because "in Adam all died" (Rom. 5:10–21; 1 Cor. 15:22). In a way we cannot fully understand, we all participated in Adam's sin. We are all accountable (Rom. 1:20–25). Yet, even in this area of personal responsibility to turn to God, there is a sense where, as Mouw says, ". . .we have often failed to recognize that sin is not necessarily sustained at every point by individual decision."[10] Analyzing Romans 1, after reading Mouw's above statement, we see that when we rebelled against God (in Adam) and suppressed the truth in (or by) unrighteousness (Rom. 1:18), God "gave us over" to degrading passions, to the lusts of our hearts, and to depraved minds (thinking). Thus, we became "filled with every kind of wickedness" (Rom. 1:29). This concept of being "given over" entails being in bondage to sin in a way that goes beyond "just saying no." Galatians 6:1 also refers to this idea using the phrase "caught up" in a sinful behavior. Lenters comments:

> The term Paul uses here to describe the phenomenon of "entrapment" by sin is especially pertinent for our discussion. The basic meaning of the verb is to "grasp" or to "seize." In the active voice, it denotes the action of "taking"; in the passive it suggests acceptance or reception from another. Its deeper meaning has the connotation of ownership or integration or assimilation into one's self. The usage in Galatians 6:1 suggests a fault into which a brother is betrayed unaware, so that it is not intentionally wrong. His entrapment becomes a condition, not an isolated event.
>
> Paul's description of being caught up in an unmanageable condition of powerlessness speaks to the dynamics of addiction. No child or young person ever plans to be an addict when he or she grows up. Yet a learned behavior becomes a habit that eventually overwhelms them—to the detriment of whatever plans they have made. Their addiction also snares people close

76

to them. The parent or spouse or employer may find himself or herself caught up in several games in relationship to the addict: protecting, denying, justifying, lying, self-pitying, dominating, or even depending on the addict's dependency. All are tentacles of the addiction syndrome which reach out and touch other people besides the addict. All are agents; all are victims.[11]

Lenters here mentions the overflow effect or generalized nature of addictive behavior. Mouw contends that as Christians we have pietistically been insensitive to the ways in which one person's entrapment or bondage can be passed on to another without his having necessarily any part or control in it. He also mentions that we neglect the societal impact of sin.

There are also ways in which societies promote addictions. Our sin begins in our individual choices, but those choices get woven in certain societal stimuli. We are surrounded by the lure to materialism, to infidelity, to harmful substances, so that our behavior is not just completely dependent on our own wills. Its relation to our choices is much more mysterious than that.[12]

We must be careful not to oversimplify a complex problem. In the West, we are prone to analyze *ad nauseum* and forget the *gestalt* or the whole. The important thing may not be so much *why* or *how* people got addicted but what they are doing about it.

It is important to remind ourselves that, biblically, sin has four main components: (1) Rebelliousness, (2) Guilt, (3) Shame, and (4) Bondage. As evangelicals, we tend to emphasize the three aspects of rebellion, guilt, and shame, but ignore bondage. The concept of being "given over" to sinful behavior and becoming "entrapped" beyond our own will and decision-making power is what bondage is all about. Not only does sin produce rebelliousness (*wanting our own way, insisting upon control*), guilt (*true moral and/or legal culpability*), and shame (*a sense of lowered self-esteem*), but it also produces bondage (*an inability to help ourselves, to extricate ourselves from entrapment*). These aspects of sin are passed on to us in four ways:[13]

(1) By means of our adamic sin nature (Rom. 1–5; 1 Cor. 15:22);

(2) Through the law of generations, that is the blessings and curses of covenant faithfulness versus covenant disobedience (Ex. 20:5; 34:7; Lev. 26:34, 39; Num. 14:33; Isa. 65:7; Amos 7:17; Jer. 16:10–11; Deut. 5:9; 1 Kings 14:9; Pss. 21:10; 22:8–9; 37:28);

(3) Through personal choice to sin, that is, the law of reaping and sowing (Gal. 6:7–8; 1 Cor. 9:11; 2 Cor. 9:6; Hos. 8:7; 10:12; Prov. 22:8–9);

(4) Through trauma from a broken, sinful world (sociological and systematic evil such as corrupt judges, wicked rulers, corrupt priests or prophets, accidents, disease, etc.).

As Mouw, Lenters, and Sweeten point out, addiction is a prime example of all aspects of sin being formed into a person's nature, and thus coming out in their daily experience. There are aspects of rebellion (idolatry), guilt, shame, and bondage in every addiction story that I have ever encountered in my clinical counseling practice.

ADDICTION: A DISEASE

Many Christians question the use of the term "disease" in regard to addictive behavior. Indeed, people in the field *do* seem to use the term rather glibly. We are used to thinking, on the other hand, of "disease" as a strictly *physically-caused* process, for example, heart disease. We think of it genetically, "Oh his family had a history of heart disease," or physically, "His heart just gave out." Yet even in the realm of what traditionally have been thought of as "merely physical" problems (e.g., heart, cancer, etc.), we are discovering psychological and spiritual dimensions. We are finding that cancer victims tend to be resentful, unforgiving people or that the type A's who have heart attacks are unusually hostile and cynical. Does this mean that they do not have a *disease?* Are not these people still *responsible* for their lifestyles that helped produce these conditions?

Rather than quibble over a word, I prefer to focus on the fact that whether there is an addictive "disease" or a "disorder" (the term I use), obviously there *are* physical, psychological, and spiritual factors involved. Also, there is a much larger issue underlying all addictive behaviors. William Lenters refers to it in his book *The Freedom We Crave: Addiction—The Human Condition,* as do Jim and Phyllis Alsdurf in their article "The Generic Disease" in *Christianity Today.* They state,

> Something need not qualify as a disease in order for it to be a legitimate and significant human concern. One cannot help wondering if the ... voices ... who tell us that almost everybody is codependent are merely describing human nature. Could codependency be that part of the human condition in which the search for connectedness and the avoidance of loneliness have gone awry? ... The ontological reality of being human is that in any attempt to avoid loneliness we may give away too much of ourselves—to a chemical substance or to an unhealthy relationship—and so experience a new form of loneliness.[14]

There is an addictive process in human nature. It has physical, spiritual, and psychological dimensions. *Anything* that becomes central to a person's functioning—whether it is drugs, alcohol, church work, money, work, food relationships—anything can become addictive. And once that process of making the activity central has begun, it becomes very difficult to make drastic changes, even when the person "knows" he should do so. Thus, the compulsive/addictive nature of these disorders.

Much energy needed to deal with the addictive process and the chaos it causes is wasted trying to "prove" that addictions are "merely" one thing or another. A more productive use of energy or resources is to recognize the multidimensional nature of the addictive process, being careful not to assign too much importance to any *one* factor alone. There seems to be a tendency in evangelical circles to want to "blame" people for things rather than help them overcome their problems. We seem to think that if we can say "It's their *fault*," then *we* are absolved of any responsibility to help or to encourage the healing process. Certain people in the scientific community seem eager to say that these disorders are "merely" physical. Some even seem to be saying that if it is physically based, then the spiritual or psychological mechanisms are irrelevant. Thankfully, not all Christians, nor all scientists, hold these "all or nothing" positions. However, we need to develop a more balanced approach to these issues.

The following case study is an illustration of how codependency feels to a person living through it. It illustrates the impact of early experience and the addictive nature of the disorder.

Anna is a thirty-five-year-old woman, married with one child. She is well educated, having two masters degrees in science. Her father and mother are in their seventies. Her dad is dying of heart disease brought on by alcoholism. Anna has two siblings, but neither of them want to talk about her dad's alcoholism. In her early twenties, Anna tried drugs, alcohol, and sex as ways to numb her inner pain. She describes her story this way:

> When you're codependent, a critical need in your past was simply not met. Until you begin to understand what you're actually doing, you spend all your waking moments trying to fix the hurt, trying to get something to suppress the pain that lingers inside of you. What causes codependency to be addictive is the hope that this inner need will someday be met.

There seems to be an absolute inner conviction that this is not the way life is supposed to be. Therefore, there must be a solution.

Certain "mommy and daddy" types *seem* to hold the promise of fulfilling that need and healing the aching void inside. "If he or she would really love me, then I'd be whole." This pursuit for an emotional connection leads to addiction to a person (or persons) in codependency. It's the dangling carrot that keeps us going. It's the hope for a solution that causes us to turn again and again to that certain person who seems to embody the fulfillment of our needs.

Since no human person can really heal our hurt, meet all our unmet needs from the past, and fill up the void inside us, these relationships are doomed to fail from the start. Sooner or later we realize "No, this is not the person. I must have been mistaken." Or, the person of our dreams lets us down or rejects us. Then we spend years blaming ourselves. We think it's all our fault, that we're defective and that's why no one can love us. Eventually someone else (or the same person) starts to show us love again. Once more, we dare to hope for our solution, that perfect person. The cycle starts all over again.

If years ago I had come to the conclusion that no one and nothing would heal this pain in me, I would have most definitely committed suicide. (I came very close many times.) It was the hope that kept me alive: hope that there was a solution, that life really wasn't supposed to be this painful. I kept looking and looking for someone or something to heal the gaping wound inside of me. I didn't even know why I hurt so badly— only that I hurt all the time with pain so intense, I wanted to die.

I used many means to suppress my pain. Primarily, I used food. I didn't know that my need had anything to do with people. It felt completely like it was a need for food. This added to the cycle of codependency because I became obese at a very young age. My family was mortified at this and told me repeatedly how ashamed they were of me. At school, I was the brunt of everyone's jokes and anger. It hurt a lot. The one time I dared to say how hurt I was, my mother yelled, "It's your own damn fault. If you weren't so damned fat, this wouldn't happen." That gave me the reason why I hurt (or so I thought). I came to believe that if I just got thin, I would be loved. But food was literally my means of surviving in my alcoholic home. I couldn't give it up. So I was caught in a no-win situation. Eventually I became anorexic and bulimic. As long as I was obsessed with food and weight, I didn't have to deal with people and pain.

To me, people represented pain and that was all. I withdrew from my family and nearly everyone else. I started to believe that I could live without anyone, that I could get rid of all my feelings. I liked plants so much more than people. They didn't hurt me. I really thought that trees were my best friends. Science became an obsession and an additional means of escape from pain. I was convinced I could become an intellectual rock with no feelings.

Eventually, this system broke down. I ultimately had to admit that I did have feelings and I did need people. Simply realizing this did not solve the problem. I still needed a lot of healing. Every time I tried to allow loving people into my life, the pain got so much more intense that I had to shut them out. My need was so intense that I overwhelmed other people and they had to shut me out, too. When I met a person who seemed able to meet my need for love, I wanted a perfectly loving, completely devoted mommy and daddy—people who would be able to give me what I had never gotten so long ago.

For a while, I thought that if I just stayed with my parents for as long as I could, I would be able to gather up enough crumbs to make up for what we never had. This seemed to hold the promise of filling up part of the void within me. I moved out of their house for the last time at age twenty-nine. Even when I went back to visit, I would cry the whole way home because I didn't want to leave them. But I knew, even then, that this was no solution. The real healing had begun, and I couldn't play games anymore.

Breaking out of codependency was difficult. The process of healing and change has been extremely painful, but no more painful than living out the cycles of codependency. Sometimes I still have twinges of infatuation when I meet a loving "mommy or daddy" type. But for the most part, I am free from the bondage of codependency. It was worth the pain!

Anna became a Christian in her late twenties, entered therapy, and over the last ten years has seen substantial healing. She has a good marriage and a new baby. Becoming a Christian was a "first step" and finding a Christian therapist was crucial. Through Christian therapy, prayer for inner healing, and her own dogged endurance, she has let go of her family and her codependency behaviors. She is presently preparing for her father's imminent death. Her previous work in therapy has made this process much less traumatic than it might have been. During her therapy, she realized that she had been a victim of sibling incest for a number of years as a small child. She began to understand why she had had all that pain that seemed to have no source. God had dramatically ministered to her through inner healing prayer in therapy. Considering that in her early experiences with therapy (she was molested by two different therapists, one male, one female), it is amazing that she had the courage to try to find a Christian therapist. Her hope that life could be better held her in good stead, and she has found a level of peace she never knew possible.

Here is another case study which will illustrate how codependency operates.

Laura is a beautiful woman in her early fifties. She is tall, with gorgeous hair, a well-proportioned body (she's a model), and a charming personality. Everyone adores her. Men flock to her wherever she goes. She dates millionaires and has more chances to socialize than she has time. Laura was married in her early thirties to Sam. They were unable to have children but seemingly had a good relationship. Then a few years ago, Laura discovered that Sam was having an affair. Once caught, he swore it was over, devoted himself to Laura, redecorated their home from top to bottom, and "wined and dined" her regularly. She was in heaven, sure of this love—then the bottom fell out. She found that he had never broken off the other relationship at all! Devastated, she filed for divorce. When she came to see me, she found it difficult not to maintain contact with him and wanted to take him back, despite the fact that we discerned he is most likely a sexual addict, and has no intention of coming back to her. Laura began dating soon after the divorce and cannot seem to stay home. She describes herself as "terrified of the loneliness" and is sure she will have severe anxiety attacks if she stays home and/or does not have "a man in my life." She recently has begun a renewal search for the spiritual values and a closer walk with God through Christ. This is her description of what codependency is like for her:

> I was shocked and devastated when I discovered that my husband was having an affair about three years ago, but I was even more devastated when he left me about one and a half years later. When I found out about the affair, we had hours of discussion, crying, and so forth. I decided to forgive him, take him back, and make the marriage wonderful. He promised never to see or communicate with her again, and to begin marriage counseling.
>
> This began eighteen months of struggle for me, and, I guess, for him also. We saw four different marriage counselors, since he didn't want to go back but would agree to see another one. During this period I devoted all my energy to trying to make the marriage work, and he pretended to be doing the same thing—flowers, gifts, loving cards, and notes when he was out of town, weekends away together and more. I always felt something wasn't just right, but when I would ask questions, he would just say it was his job situation. (He was in management for a large company that was having great financial problems and massive lay-offs for the previous four years.) After one year and two months of "working on our marriage and having it get better and better" according to him, I found out the "other woman" was still in the picture and that he had never given her up. (She lived in another state, and he only saw her three or four times during the period, so he says, but they talked on the

phone every day.) I should have learned a lesson but I didn't. Again, we decided to see another marriage counselor and make one last effort to save the marriage, or at least I made the commitment. I realize now that he wasn't serious about saving the marriage but was more interested in staying with me to save his job. He was eventually laid off after eighteen years with the company, and I feel this was the last straw for him. He was a workaholic, and his job and success financially meant everything to him.

After he left, I sat and cried for about three weeks. I felt my life was over. I finally decided I wasn't going to let two people destroy my life so I lectured myself for an entire weekend and began a new approach to life.

The next year was spent running, running, running. I thought I would never have a date, felt I was unattractive, stupid, had a bad body—otherwise, my husband wouldn't have left. My friends kept saying to me to look in the mirror because I was just the opposite of how I perceived myself at that time. I was surprised when I was asked out for my first date. This was only the beginning as I dated many men and turned down many. I had proven one point: I was attractive to the opposite sex. But I was still very unhappy and could not stand the thought of being alone. I hated those "awful feelings" when I was home alone and when I did not have a "special man" in my life.

At the end of the first year of being alone and still not having found anyone I wanted to spend my life with, I decided to seek counseling from Dr. Rinck. During this year I had read a lot of self-help books, and I felt several were the history of my life, especially those dealing with women who love too much and codependency. Dr. Rinck suggested I give up all men and not date for six months. I could not imagine doing this for six days let alone six months. She said she felt I had an addiction to love and men (not sex) and that I would always choose men who have problems, are emotionally unavailable, emotionally ill, workaholics, or have drinking problems—people I need to nurture, change, fix, help. I am strong in some areas of my life but very weak when it involves a relationship with a special

85

man. I also have a problem saying no to family, close friends, neighbors, and others.

I just could not imagine going without a date for six months but decided I would give it a try. I lasted three weeks and started seeing a "friend" I had met and danced with from time to time during the past six months. I thought that I could have "men friends" but, you guessed it, it was not long until romance began creeping into the relationship. I knew from the beginning it could never work and that this would never begin to fulfill my expectations of what I wanted in a beautiful marriage. I became "hooked into this person" because of my addiction to love and the codependency. I am in the process of getting out of the relationship, but it is a real struggle because I am terrified of being alone and having to face my feelings.

I now know Dr. Rinck is correct. I tried it my way, and it has not worked. I am finally realizing I have to be alone for a period of time to work on me and learn to love me fully before I can be healthy enough to choose a man who is also secure and healthy. I must face my feelings, work through them and let them go, I can no longer live in the past, nor in the future, but in the "now." I must break the codependency cycle by being alone and learning who I am and what I want. By doing this, I will no longer let someone else control me, but I will be in control of my life and I will also know I cannot control another person.

6
THE CYCLE OF CODEPENDENCY

So far we've looked at what codependent behavior is. Now we need to see its cycle—how it is maintained.

Codependent behavior is learned behavior. It is perpetrated by four primary factors:

(1) Faulty and irrational emotional habits
(2) Reinforcement of faulty past conditioning
(3) Spiritual disobedience
(4) Manipulation

While there may be many individual influences and factors that contribute to a particular man or woman's codependency, they usually fall into one of these four groups.

FAULTY BELIEF SYSTEMS

All of us possess a repertoire of irrational beliefs about life which we learned as children. I have found that codependent people have certain beliefs in common. The people I have worked with possess strikingly similar core beliefs about relationships. Claudia Black,[1] Janet Woititz,[2] Sharon Wegsheider-Cruse,[3] and many other clinicians and researchers have written extensively about the "relationship myths" with which codependent people grow up. The following is a representative list of such myths:

(1) **If I get close to someone, agree with someone, or do what they want me to do, I will lose my identity or sense of self. I will cease to be a separate person.**

In some ways codependent people learned this one from experience. Often in a dysfunctional family, getting close to someone does mean losing your own identity. In families where members are "enmeshed" with one another, the boundaries between people are blurred. It becomes difficult to know who is who and who needs what. Boundaries are the physical and emotional safety zones around each person. To give a simple example of physical boundaries with which we all have some experience: If you have ever been to a party and met someone else who stood within twelve inches of your face, you probably felt uncomfortable. That person invaded your space, crossed your physical boundaries. Americans seem to prefer eighteen to twenty-four inches of personal physical space when in casual conversations. Latinos, on the other hand, prefer a much closer physical proximity when in communication. This simple example of a physical boundary shows that it is a learned rule that can vary from culture to culture or family to family.

All of us have physical and emotional boundary needs, but not all of us were taught how to maintain the emotional space needed. If family members were too intrusive (as we discussed under "boundary violations" in chapter 4), then we can learn that either we are not entitled to boundaries or that we need immense ones to be safe. People who learned to build immense boundaries find it difficult to get close for the same reason. They fear if their boundaries come down, they will come all the way down and they will lose their personhood. Some people were so dominated and controlled as children that they either comply and agree totally with everyone about everything or they go to the other extreme and resist, disagree with, and reject everything and everyone. The people who comply/agree all the time never knew it was okay to disagree. Parents and authority figures were so powerful and seemingly all-knowing—how could you disagree with them? Especially when they said *God* was on their side? So the boundaries came down (or never went up) and Mom and Dad's views became their children's views with little or no personal ownership. These are people who at twenty-five or thirty years of age find themselves "going through the motions" in their Christian faith—doing and saying the "right things" but feeling very empty inside.[4]

The individuals who go to the other extreme and resist everything have the fear that they will lose their integrity if they go along with *anything* someone else needs or wants. Dominated for so long as children and told that their opinions, needs, wants, desires, were unimportant, these women and men decide that to preserve their selfhood, they have to resist, disagree, object to, and negate all outside inputs. They have not learned that they can agree or comply and still be separate people.

For these people, the myth of closeness and lost personhood is no myth at all. They acutely experience the threat of the myth at a deep emotional level. The problem for them is that they have never experienced what a healthy functional relationship was like. They do not know that they can agree, comply, or get close and yet maintain their separateness and integrity. Codependents who accept this myth struggle with over-control and often are sexually nonorgasmic in their intimate relationships or experience erectile dysfunction.

(2) Couples do everything together. We will be one.

People who believe this one suffer from compulsion. They are still yearning for that oneness none of us can ever achieve again—oneness with Mother in the womb. They are looking for another to completely fulfill their every need, make them whole, and heal them. While all of us yearn for that oneness to some extent, these people do so with an unhealthy

89

compulsion. Healthy people learn to let go of, give up, and free, that which they love in order to grow up. If for some reason a child does not get beyond this stage and stays stuck in separation anxiety, problems relating to others will be maintained in adult life. People who still experience fear and anxiety unless connected to others, as we said earlier, tend to fall in love hard and fast, and experience the normal post-infatuation stage of the relationship as rejection. Then, they either cling to the other with great ferocity or abandon him.

Darlene and David got married while in college. Actually, they had been living together and became converts to Christianity through a campus Christian ministry. So they decided to do the "right thing" and formalize their relationship. Darlene was delighted because her first months as a new Christian had been difficult, and now she assumed that she and David would do everything together. *Now that he is committed to me,* she thought, *I'll never have to pray alone or study the Bible alone. We'll do everything together!* Did she have a shock!

(3) If people really get to know the "real" me, they will reject me and abandon me. So I will have to be one person inside and someone else on the outside.

This belief stems from deep feelings of unworthiness and shame. Being perfectionists and longing to be unique, these people are sure that they will never measure up. One client recently told me how an older sibling had always gotten good grades, while she herself had struggled. At last in college, she decided to prove herself to her dad, who had repeatedly told her, "Joanie's the good girl. I can count on her. You're a disappointment to me." So first semester she got four A's and one B. Dad looked at her grades and said, "So what's with the B?" So next time she tried harder. She got all A's. Now she was certain that she would get the praise for which she had longed. Her father stared blankly at the grade report and said, "Oh well, you're in elementary education—that's pretty easy stuff!" Even though this incident had occurred years ago, my client was devastated and wept profusely as she recounted the incident.

Many codependent people feel as if they are two people: the inner self and the phony outer self. Even when the outer self looks good, is successful, well-groomed, talented, does well socially or professionally, many do not "accept" that self as the "real self." As children they felt that they had to conceal their true self, their true feelings, and their true thoughts. As a result, these individuals automatically behave according to what they think other people want from them. Inside, they still feel like the emotionally neglected little child—weak and vulnerable. Since their inner self was ridiculed, ignored, or unacceptable when they were children, it never occurs to them that others will—now that they have grown up—react differently than parents and other early-life authority figures. So they remain frightened and in despair. They want closeness and long to be "real," but they are too terrified to try. Being vulnerable and taking a risk to share honestly always seemed to have had "terrible" consequences as a child, so they assume the same thing will happen now.

Unfortunately, sometimes in the Christian community, taking interpersonal risks, being open with one's fears, foibles, and fantasies is not without consequences. One client, a new Christian, recently told me that she and her husband prefer to attend AA or Al-Anon meetings for fellowship and sharing because "at church we've noticed that people look shocked, withdraw, and stop talking to us when we say something about our struggles, fears, and doubts. At least at AA everyone comes admitting they are in trouble, and no one is trying to pretend they are okay, like they do at church." This statement is a sad indictment of the Christian church as a loving, healing community, yet I have heard it repeated many times by Christian believers who are new to the church or are new to the process of Twelve Step Recovery.

(4) "Anything that goes wrong is my fault. I'm a worthless

person, incapable of doing things right. If my partner is unhappy it is because I have failed at my job as a spouse."

This myth locks people into shame-bound behavior patterns (see figure 3). In a strange way, believing I am to blame for everything is a way to stay in control. The unconscious rationale is this: "If I am at fault, then I can fix it. If something is wrong because of me, then I can change it." To acknowledge that the other person is in charge of his own feelings and happiness feels too out of control. Codependent people like to feel they can fix things, solve problems, eliminate conflict. If the problem belongs to someone else, how can they fix it? So there is a payoff for blaming oneself—remaining in control of the situation.

Blaming oneself also leads to a guilt-ridden and shame-oriented self-image. This leads to self-destructive behavior as a "punishment." Ruth Ellen blames herself for Ralph's distance and indifference. She thinks that if she were sexier, thirty pounds lighter (she's not really overweight), more intelligent, and a "better" cook, then he would be kinder to her. She is generous with her children and has no problem buying them things that they need or want. Yet she has not had a new dress for three years. She tells herself she "doesn't deserve" nice things, so even when the children buy her perfume or a new blouse, she exchanges it for something "for the house." Often by focusing on imagined faults or taking the blame even when not at fault, codependent people end up ignoring their real problems. They spend so much energy defending against or making up for their supposed faults, that they fail to uncover and deal with more basic problems. They ignore their people-pleasing, overly compliant behavior; self-righteousness; judgmental attitudes; compulsive behaviors (like overeating or workaholism); temper tantrums; pouting; and other manipulative behaviors. Taking the victim's stance, they do not recognize that playing victim can be a very controlling maneuver. If nothing else, it generates a lot of self-pity! And of course, it helps maintain low self-esteem.

(5) **"Happy couples never have conflict, argue, or criticize one another. They never take each other for granted; always cherish one another, and never feel angry with one another."**

When people believe this myth, they do so because they assume that validation from others is crucial for living, and that only agreement produces such validation. They do not allow conflict nor do they have adequate problem-solving skills. They look to others for validation of their feelings, beliefs, and thoughts—indeed, for their very being! If someone disagrees with them, they feel rejected. They take other people's feelings or thoughts as personal attacks against them. They unconsciously believe that love and anger are incompatible: "If you are angry with me, you do not love me." The flip side of this situation can occur in a conflict when they sometimes turn on the other person as if to say: "I can't control or contain my own anger (I'm too afraid of it), so I must reject or alienate you." Rather than even allow themselves to experience their anger, they tell themselves that it is too dangerous to feel it, so they will reject the other person before too much of the anger leaks out.

One client told me that he was shocked to read in a book about marriage that you had to work at it! He assumed that successful marriages just happen! Another young man in his twenties told me that he genuinely believed that he could go out with "the boys" four to five nights a week, work sixty hours a week at his job, and that somehow his marriage would "just happen"—without any special effort or nurturing on his part. Neither of these individuals had faced the inevitable conflicts that are part of a relationship when two people live together in marriage. They assumed that no matter how they acted their spouse would still respond lovingly to their behavior, never criticize or find fault with them, or feel angry! When someone tells me, "Oh my spouse and I *never fight or argue*," I always wonder which one of them is dead!

REINFORCEMENT OF FAULTY
PAST CONDITIONING

So we see that codependent behavior is maintained by faulty beliefs and assumptions, especially regarding relationships. Codependent behavior is also maintained by reinforcement of faulty conditioning from the past. Although it may seem complicated, reinforcement is a simple concept to understand. If, for example, every time the baby cries Mother comes running to the infant, she reinforces the child's behavior. The baby learns that making those shrill sounds and waving his arms and legs around will bring Mother running. If every time your dog growls, you pat him on the head and say in a soothing voice, "There, there Bowser, it's okay. You don't need to growl," you reinforce your dog's growling. He learns that his behavior will generate a pleasant soothing response from his master. When we provide a positive or reinforcing response to an action, we increase the likelihood that a behavior will be repeated. This is true even if we do not consciously intend to produce certain behaviors in our children, pets, or others around us. We have all seen parents who unwittingly reinforce "cry-baby" behavior in their child by making a huge fuss over the child's every minor scrape or bruise. The child is a quick learner and develops the habit of crying loudly over minor incidents because he knows Mom or Dad will come running!

The same powerful conditioning of behavior applies to our faulty learning from the past. If as a child, Mary learned that the people close to her (Mom, Dad, her brothers, and sisters) were apt to give double-bind messages to one another within the family, she will learn that this is the communication pattern in intimate interpersonal relationships. She will not, therefore, question this same behavior in boyfriends or in her husband. Double-bind messages are messages that say two or more opposing things at once.[5] For example, "Sit down and stand up!" or "Of course I love you, now go away and quit

FIGURE 7

DOUBLEBIND MESSAGES FROM CHILDHOOD

Adapted from Struggle For Intimacy, J. G. Woitiz (1985)

Childhood Message	Adult Response
1. "I love you/Go away." "Be near me/Go away."	1. Chooses friends who are cold and distant one minute, loving the next. Selects companions who are unreliable, who do one thing but say another thing.
2. "I need you/ You can't do anything right."	2. Attracted to people who "need you" but who are nasty to you, too. Drawn to partners who are both critical and dependent. Keeps seeking approval from others who are not apt to give it.
3. "Yes, so and so does and says those awful things. But you must UNDERSTAND!! He/she was just — (drunk, sick, tired, busy ...)."	3. Becomes the world's <u>most</u> "understanding" person even in the face of abuse. Makes excuses for others, but rarely gives himself the same grace or allowances. Blames self for problems in relationships.
4. "I promise, I'll be there for you - next time!"	4. Learns not to need things, so as to not be disappointed. Wants others to read his mind as to what he needs and wants. Complains that he has to "do everything" in this relationship." Abdicates his personal responsibility for his own happiness. Tends to believe others' words while ignoring their actions.
5. "Don't worry, Dear. Everything is just fine. It's going to be all right./Oh my gosh, how I can I handle this mess?"	5. Becomes a "Super Person." Acts overly responsible, rescues others. Caretakes others who are needy whether they want it or not. Takes charge inappropriately.

bothering me." Children who receive these types of messages get used to being confused. Thus, in adult life they are apt to choose friends who are nice, friendly, and warm today, but cool or rude tomorrow. Or, they will date others who promise things but do not follow through. The promise says "Come close, I care," while the lack of follow-through says "Go away."

Figure 7 lists a number of examples of double-bind messages, which codependent people can usually identify in their backgrounds. The effect of these early messages is this: These people, unaware of these old beliefs, unconsciously react to them, and in so doing, inadvertently draw to themselves people who reinforce the old belief. You see, they focus on what is familiar. So if, for example, they learned that people say with their mouth that they love them, while at the same time these persons act in an emotionally or physically abusive way, then they tend to look unconsciously for relationships and situations that will fulfill this pattern of how things "should be" and for things that "feel familiar."

Consider Joe, a bright, actually brilliant, young man. His father committed suicide when Joe was eight or nine years old. All of his father's relatives say that his mother killed his father, but there was never any proof. Joe's father was an alcoholic and so was his mother. From early on, Joe learned to care for his mother and siblings. He would pack their lunches and get the younger ones off to school. When his mother got drunk, he would nurse her back to sobriety. Joe had legitimate needs: playing, relaxing, or being cared for himself. These needs were rarely, if ever, considered so Joe learned never to expect anything for himself. He discovered, as a result, that whenever he got close to accomplishing a goal, he would somehow manage to sabotage it. When he finished his course work for his Ph.D., he had a car wreck and was unable to work on the dissertation. By the time he recovered, it seemed to him that it was "too late" to pick up where he had left off. One time he had a chance to work for a prestigious company at triple the salary he was earning, doing "grunt work" for a local realtor. The company had heard of him, called him, and asked to review his resumé. It took him six weeks to get the resumé together. His comment to me was "I felt like I was lying—that I could not be as good as my resumé said I was. I wonder if I even *deserve* such a good job. . .even though I *know* I really *am* qualified."

Another client came in recently and told me a similar story. In her family, loyalty is a very important issue, as it is in many families. Amanda was the oldest daughter, and although she had older male siblings, the caretaking role fell to her. She explained that in her cultural group, this custom was very common. Dutifully, she would come home after school, watch the babies, clean the house, cook dinner, bathe the younger kids, and so on. Often Mom and Dad were gone, even for one or two days in a row. They would leave Amanda completely in charge of the house. Needless to say, no one ever asked Amanda if she wanted all this responsibility. She was not asked if her own needs were being met. When her parents returned home, her father was usually drunk and Mom sat on the couch and expected to be waited on hand and foot by Amanda. So Amanda learned that it was her role to finish school and then to stay at home to care for her parents.

One day in school, some high school friends were talking about what they planned to do after graduation. Some planned to go away to college; others intended to join the military service; still others wanted to find a job and get their own apartment. Amanda was literally aghast! She asked them, "What do you mean? Children are supposed to grow up and stay home and care for their parents!" Her friends laughed at her for being so naive! Such was her understanding and entrance into the real world. Amanda didn't even know that she had any choices or rights to make plans for her own future and livelihood. She thought her only choice was the one that her family had taught and trained her to fulfill.

Now, some twenty-five years later, she is breaking away

from these old beliefs, but it is difficult. For the last twenty-five years she has been in a convent. The experience of living as a member of a religious order has turned out to be much like living at home with her mother. Recently she has made some independent choices for herself. She is going to graduate school on a scholarship, has moved into her own apartment, and has obtained a part-time job. She has stopped her binge eating, lost weight, and begun to improve her social skills—all until this past month. Just as she was finishing her last quarter of the year's schooling, receiving positive evaluations at work, getting compliments for improved appearance, she started to experience severe anxiety attacks. Then she started to binge eat and feel very discouraged!

When Amanda came in to see me, we discussed the loyalty issue. In her family loyalty means "believing what the family believes." I asked Amanda what her family believed about her success. She recognized right away that the family script for her was that she was "a dumb girl who would never amount to anything." Thus, when she began to run counter to the family script and began to experience some success, Amanda began to experience a deep conflict: "Should I be loyal to my family's beliefs about me (and sabotage my success) or can I break away from their script for me and find some new way to be loyal to them?" She was not consciously aware of this inner battle, but she was able to recognize it once we began to talk about her difficulties. So now she is trying to discover a new way to be loyal to her family without having to accept their beliefs about her.

Both Joe and Amanda were responding to what was familiar to them: loyalty to the family script regarding success and failure, and loyalty to the family script about what they did and didn't deserve to get out of life. Codependent people need to understand the faulty conditioning from their past so that they can relearn how to respond positively to present life experiences.

So far we've seen how codependency is maintained by

(1) faulty beliefs and irrational emotional habits; (2) reinforcement of faulty past conditioning. Now we will examine a third factor: spiritual disobedience.

SPIRITUAL DISOBEDIENCE

In chapter 5 we looked at how addictive behaviors may be seen at their core to be a form of idolatry. The person or thing to which the individual is addicted becomes the addict's central focus in life. No longer is his life based upon God's grace and plan, but rather on his relationship to the addictive experience. We also noted that addiction flows out of a shame state in which we humans find ourselves. Addiction becomes one way of distracting ourselves from our state of shame. It is a way that we can hide from ourselves and from our God.

There are other spiritual dynamics at work in addictive behaviors, particularly in relationship addictions. In addition to the shame state and idolatry these dynamics include:[6]

(1) **Covetousness.** Codependent people covet something or someone which God has not given them. Even in marriage, while husband and wife are spiritually one, they are not meant to possess one another's soul, being, or personality. Rather, each person maintains his unique being and enriches the marital union by bringing that being to the relationship.

Many codependents, however, become fearful when others are too distinct or different from them. It is as if the other person's distinctiveness is a negative critique of oneself. It's almost as if the codependent believes that there is only one right way to be or to do something, and so, if someone chooses a way distinct from his, one of them *must* be wrong. Since the codependent does not allow himself to be less than perfect (or so he thinks), he assumes that it would be catastrophic (i.e., he would be found to be worthless) if he was wrong. Thus, in his view, the other person must be the one who is wrong and, therefore, must become like the codependent.

Codependents covet control over other people. They want to change others, mold others, make others into the image that they think is "best" for them. In some ways, it is as if they covet the power to run other people's lives. But "for their own good" of course. Covetousness also manifests itself in the person who cannot let the other (spouse) alone physically.

This type of covetousness is seen in the couple who say they "do everything" together, with no outside friends or interests. It is as if they are trying to be one person rather than two people who are together. After a while, one even begins answering and speaking for the other. These people are using one another to fill up an emptiness in themselves—a truly symbiotic relationship!

(2) **Rebellion.** Codependent people are spiritually rebellious. Their need to be in control, to be in charge, the tendency to be furious or depressed when they cannot be, and their obsession with being "right" and perfect are all signs of spiritual rebellion. Obviously this spiritual rebellion has mental, emotional, interpersonal, and even physical effects in their daily lives. While *all* human beings are in rebellion against God (Rom. 1), codependent people seem to have a special problem with it. They do not want to "let go and let God" or let go and let anyone else. Life usually felt so out of control for them as children that they find it extremely difficult to trust God enough to let go. Often their image or view of God has been seriously distorted by an unfortunate human model: their own fathers. We tend as human beings to project onto God our Father in heaven, the same characteristics of our human fathers. For example, German theologians of the early twentieth century all seemed to see God as powerful, yet distant. They rarely spoke of a personal faith or warm relationship with the Father. When you read their works, you get the feeling that *maybe* once in your life you might make contact, but that usually the best you could do was take a leap of faith and hope that in the end God heard you. Sheila Fabricant, a popular Roman Catholic religious

worker, noted this fact about the German theologians and commented on it to a seminary professor's wife. The woman's husband was of that era in Germany, and himself a theologian. She commented that, in her view, the reason they viewed God as austere and far away was because when they were infants, the prevailing view of child care was that you never picked up a baby when it cried. You let it scream and holler, because otherwise you would "spoil it." Thus, these men learned that when they were in need, when they were hurting, when they wanted comfort, no one came. When the caretaker did come, it seemed arbitrary and in no way connected to what they needed!

Many codependent people, because of their early life experiences, also have difficulty seeing God as caring for them, loving them, being ready to help them. Thus, life seems out of control, so what they value most in life is control. All of us have what the author of Hebrews calls "besetting sins," and for codependents theirs is an extra measure of rebellion and the need to control. If I need to control everything, I am surely not going to let God be in control if I can help it. While this rebellion is bred out of *fear*, it is nonetheless rebellion!

(3) **Mistrust.** Closely related to rebellion for codependent people is mistrust. Since they mistrust God, they need to control, and hence, they rebel. They tend to be a lot like Abraham in some of his less admirable moments. Like Abraham, they have trouble believing God is capable and willing to keep His promises without their help! Abraham waited a while to see if Sarah could have a child, but when it did not happen, he decided to give God a helping hand by having intercourse with Sarah's maidservant Hagar. Codependent people are a lot like that—believing that even God needs their assistance, so they stick their oar in where it does not belong. And like Abraham, they find that their meddling can have long-term results!

Many codependent people have legitimate concerns regarding loved ones, friends, or themselves. They want to bring these matters to God in prayer. Yet often these prayers may have a compulsive frantic tone to them, as if they have to impress God with their intensity or with the quantity of their intercessions. Rather than approaching God as our loving Father who desires to give good things to His children, they approach Him as if they have to wheedle, cajole, or beg Him for help or blessings. In many ways their prayers are merely an extension of their worrying and fretting. Their prayers might sound like this:

> Oh, dear Lord—*please* help so and so. They need You, oh God! They are doing such and such, and I am so concerned for them. Protect them—ple-e-ease! Don't let anything bad happen! I *beg* You, oh God to help me and to help them! You have *promised* to help us; now You *must*! What if such and such happens! Oh Lord, I could not stand it! *Ple-e-ease do* something! I can't live without them! You must help me! Please, please, please!

These types of prayers do not come out of a heart that rests in God's sovereignty or trusts His heart of love. These types of prayers are prayed intensely, with much fervor (and resulting exhaustion) and with great frequency. While I don't mean to discount the importance of consistency in prayer (praying "without ceasing"), I think the type of prayer I've just described is really sanctified worrying! In my counseling with people, I try to help them distinguish between concern and worry. Concern is the anxiety or tension we face about something we *can* control. Worry is the anxiety and tension we experience when something in our life is out of our control.

For example, if I am concerned that I have gained ten pounds since the holidays, I can exercise, change my diet, and lose some weight. My concern and decision to act on the concern results in positive action. Worry is fretting over what I cannot control: like whether it will rain on my child's graduation party or whether the Russians will bomb New York. If something is in my control, I can do what I can do, and that's that. No worry develops. If a circumstance is beyond my control, then the biblical response is to "let go and let God." We are to give over our worries to God, because if situations are beyond our control, they are certainly within His control! So worry is unnecessary and unproductive. Thus my prayer would be more like this:

> Oh Lord, I recognize Your greatness and power and that, though it is not within my control to fix—or help so and so, it is within Your hand. I let go of so and so and place them in Your hand. I release them to You: Not my will but Yours be done. I refuse to fret and worry about this person or this situation. I trust you to take care of this person better even than I could imagine. Thank you for your grace. Amen.

How different the tone of this prayer from the preceding one. There is no cajoling, begging, or wheedling. Just a humble trust in God's grace and love. Often, we believers are so busy trying to "persuade" God about how appropriate it would be if He granted our desires, that we forget to let go of our demands and worries. We do not really trust Him to do the "right" thing. Codependent people seem to have the same need to manipulate God that they have in their relationships with other people. They seem to believe that if they are "good" and "follow the rules" then God somehow "owes them one"! Certainly, there is precedent in Scripture for petitioning God's favor, praying without ceasing, and for diligence and consistency in prayer. Yet to pray compulsively and frantically out of fear strikes me as not exactly what the apostle Peter had in mind when he said: "Humble yourselves, therefore, under God's mighty hand, that he may lift you up in due time. Cast all your anxiety on him because he cares for you" (1 Peter 5:6–7).

Codependent people need to learn to become more trusting and less controlling—even in their prayers and in their

103

relationship with God! This change in attitude can only happen when they understand that God as their loving Father truly cares for them and understands their needs, their pain, and their petitions.

MANIPULATION

The fourth way codependent behavior is maintained is through manipulation. Rentzel defines manipulation as *"attempting to control people or circumstances through deceptive or indirect means."*[7]

Manipulative behavior is insidious, subtle, seductive, and treacherous. Rentzel[8] gives a number of examples of how manipulation is used to maintain the codependent relationship. I have also noticed various ways clients I see use manipulation to maintain their relationships. It should be noted that many of the following behaviors, while innocent or even positive in themselves, can be harmful when used by a codependent person to manipulate another person or situation. Not everyone who does these things is codependent, by any means, but if there is an overall codependent pattern of behavior *plus* these behaviors in someone's life, watch out! The following are illustrative of manipulative behaviors.

Finances

Many times codependent people get sucked into rescuing someone else financially, even when they themselves are not really able to do it. Although they are unaware of it, they are really trying to buy someone's love, or keep someone from abandoning them. For example, Marlene buys her boyfriend, Harry, tires for his car, even though she knows her rent is due in ten days and she cannot afford to do so. Joe gives Oletha two hundred dollars a month just to spend frivolously, hoping to impress her with his generosity. Mary Anne lets her alcoholic brother Al move in with her and supports him, even though she knows that he will never go out and get a job while he is still drinking. Mom and Dad bail Jerry out of another financial mess, despite the fact that he gambles compulsively and cannot seem to find a steady job.

Lynette goes to work to support the family while her husband Randy tries to "find himself." Although Lynette would rather stay home with their child, she packs the baby off to day-care and works forty-five hours a week, in addition to running their home. She figures if she does this long enough, her self-sacrifice and love for Randy will be enough to inspire him on to greater accomplishments. Besides, she is afraid that if she demands he go to work, he will kill himself, because he is already very depressed. Mother and Dad buy Janet a home, furnish it with expensive antiques, oriental rugs, and a lot of art work. They feel sorry for her because she "got pregnant and had to get married," and then her husband left her. They do not insist that she find a job, and, instead, they pay for college classes for her, and also give her a monthly stipend. They seem afraid to let her grow up on her own.

Gifts, Cards, Possessions

Gifts and cards in a healthy relationship can be a wonderful way to show love and affection. For codependent people, however, they are a way to manipulate the other person into liking them or staying connected. They are given not out of altruism or unconditional love, but out of fear and a need to make the other person emotionally dependent. Sally was dating Jonathan. She was impressed that such a successful, wealthy doctor would be interested in her. Later when in treatment, she told me that she had written dozens of little love notes and slipped them into various drawers and containers in his home. She would write poetry, cards, letters and go out at 1 a.m. to the post office annex to mail them so he would get them the next day, despite having to get up at 5 a.m. herself.

Sally felt totally outclassed by Jonathan and wanted desperately to show him she was devoted to him. He hated the style of her dress (casual, sporty) and she acquiesced right away and began to purchase more sophisticated, dramatic clothing. She became obsessed with purchasing little cards, gifts, and tokens of affection for him. When not purchasing them, she was planning when and where to buy them. Jonathan, for his part, was an egotist, and ate up all this adoration. Until she came into treatment, it never occurred to Sally that her behavior was manipulative or done out of fear.

Physical Affection

Again, in a healthy, loving relationship physical affection is a very important ingredient! All of us need physical affection—and most of us do not get enough. The problem in a codependent relationship is that this normal need is exploited for personal gain. The codependent person is usually enthralled with someone who is *less* enthralled with them. The codependent wants to win the less enamored person over. So they use various affectionate ploys. It starts with nonverbal contact like staring at the other person or giving "meaningful glances" and moves along to hugs ("brotherly" or "sisterly" of course) to neck or back rubs, roughhousing, arm wrestling, tickling, and so on.

Even in marriage, affection (and sex) can be used to manipulate. If you are angry with someone, an easy way to communicate it is to refuse eye contact or to move away when the other person touches you. If someone is mad at you, then a back rub or a mock boxing match, or a hug can be used to persuade them not to be angry, even though things have not been talked out.

The Cycle of Codependency

Language

Flattery, "inside" jokes, secrets between the two people, flirting, or teasing all are ways to manipulate a relationship. Roberta says to her husband, "I just don't know what I'd do without you. I could never make it on my own. I need you so much." Sam leans over to Joanna and whispers, "But honey, you can't break up with me. You are the only one in the world who understands me." Andrea says to Tom: "Now, honey-babe, don't go talking like that! You know there's no one else in this world for me! You're my little honey-babe, I couldn't let *you* go." Stanley says to Alexandra: "Now this will be our little secret. No one else will know that you had the abortion. We'll keep it between us, and as long as we're together, no one else will suspect."

Emotional Dishonesty

Many codependent relationships are based on emotional dishonesty. Negative feelings or thoughts are suppressed, denied, or repressed. Differences are glossed over and ignored. Mandy comes from an upper-class family. Her dad is a professor and her mom a well-known charity volunteer. Brilliant herself, Mandy has been influential in social action causes around the state. She has put her wit, charm, and wisdom to work in numerous projects, speaking engagements, and media appearances. Mandy was married quite young, had four children, and then lost her husband to alcoholism. Absolutely devoted to him, Mandy was devastated when he died in a drunken stupor as his car hit a retaining wall at one hundred m.p.h. She went into therapy and discovered that despite her own good qualities, she had always relied on male approval for her sense of well-being. Her dad, while benign in many ways, was also aloof and emotionally unavailable. So she constantly sought his approval, and that of her late husband. While in therapy, Mandy met a wealthy politician named Larry who wined and dined

107

her and swept her off her feet. A lawyer, this man had lots of charm, money, and power, but their lifestyles could not have been more different! He liked fast cars; ostentatious jewelry and clothes; bragged about being born again; hated literature and the arts; decorated his home in glass and chrome; and only associated with people who "understood" him. Mandy, on the other hand, loved literature, drama, the arts; homemaking, crafts, country living, barbecues, and picnics; decorated her small home in a relaxed country style; was quiet about her faith; and had friends from every social strata. Also, Larry disliked children, was a fanatic about cleanliness, and hated pets. Mandy and her four kids were crazy about pets, loved to live in a relaxed fashion, and always had swarms of neighborhood children in the house.

As the relationship grew more serious, Mandy began to question Larry's beliefs and lifestyle. He became very defensive and insisted that if they were going to date, she would have to do things his way. A great charmer, he persuaded Mandy to become engaged, despite her doubts. During her last therapy session, she said to me: "I know that I am running after a dream, an illusion. But Larry treats me much better than my late husband did. Even if I have to suppress myself, pretend I like glass and chrome, wear fancy clothes I dislike, ignore my interests in art and literature, and live a lie, it is better than being a widow with four kids. I find it almost impossible to believe that God could meet my needs without this man in my life. I need Larry's love and approval so much. I know it is foolish, but I can't say 'no' to him."

Here was a situation where someone decided it was easier to be emotionally dishonest in order to keep someone in her life, than to be herself and risk losing him.

Game-Playing

Another way codependency is maintained in a relationship is through game-playing. Game-playing is not unique to codependent relationships, but seems to be a necessary ingredient. Game-playing can be spotted in phrases like these:

"I guess you'll stop being my friend *now.*"

"I would have come over to see you, but I knew you would have been too busy to visit with *me.*"

"I guess you wish God had given you a different mother."

"If you really loved me, you'd. . ."

"I guess all I can do is go off somewhere and die."

"Well, all I can do now is find another church where the pastor will understand me."

"That's right. Yell at me. *I* can never do *anything* right."

"If you leave me, I'll have no other choice but to kill myself. I can't live without you."

Game-playing can also be seen where people pout, brood, or withdraw into angry silence. "What's wrong honey?" "Nothing (sigh)." People who provoke insecurity in others are also playing games. For example, someone who threatens to leave the relationship when they know their spouse is terrified of being abandoned, or someone who knows their spouse is sensitive about weight yet still makes remarks about how attractive other people are in comparison. Undermining the relationships your friend or spouse has with other people is another way to play games and manipulate. Ways this is usually done are these: becoming friends with the other person yourself so your spouse has to share the relationship with you; implying that your friend or spouse is weird for even wanting this other person for a friend; telling them that their other friend(s) "do not really care like *I* do. No one can care for you like *I* do."; embarrassing your spouse or friend when they are with you and their other friend(s), so that they will hesitate to go out with them again.

Playing Victim

Codependent people have the knack of being very strong and controlling, and yet they are able to play victim at the drop of a hat! One minute they can solve everyone's dilemmas (if only people would listen), but the next, they are helpless and totally dependent. This characteristic stems from their "all or nothing" mentality: "Either I am able to control everything or I cannot handle anything." Thus, whenever it is convenient, codependent people can switch from Superperson to Victim without so much as a costume change. They are experts at creating or exaggerating problems to gain sympathy, attention, or help. Yet, ironically, often when real help is offered, they refuse it because it would mean an end to the codependent relationship. This is why many codependent women seek help to get out of one bad relationship, only to fall back into the arms of the next bum to come along!

Christine was married three times over the last twenty-five years. One husband was a misogynist (a man who hates women) and the other two were alcoholics. When she entered therapy, she was attempting to break off a relationship with a man who was also an alcoholic. Over the next year, she dedicated her life to Christ, began to go to Al-Anon, continued in therapy, and finally broke off the relationship. For six months, all went well. She attended church, support groups, retreats, and therapy sessions. Then at Christmas, she began to feel shaky. Her kids were all away so she was alone for the first time. Despite some healthy relationships with women available to her, Christine "forgot" to plan for this extra stress of loneliness. Enter Jack: a recovering alcoholic, misogynist, and con man. Jack had dated Christine's sister some years earlier, but Christine only knew him casually. Now, through a mutual interest in a charity, she and Jack were seeing each other quite a bit. Before she knew it, Christine was finding herself entangled, and being pressured to marry Jack! She knew she did not want to marry him but was afraid to break it off because she didn't want to "hurt" him. She was playing the victim once again.

SUMMARY

We have seen that codependency is maintained by four main factors: (1) faulty belief and irrational emotional habits; (2) reinforcement of faulty past conditioning; (3) spiritual disobedience; and (4) manipulation. In chapter 7 we will discuss how to recover from codependency.

7

BREAKING THE CYCLE OF CODEPENDENCY

Recovery. Yes, you can recover from a lifestyle of codependency. Is it easy? No. Is it quick? No. Is it once for all? No. Recovery is a process—an ongoing, lifelong process. You never totally recover because the habits are strong and the predisposing factors are still within, but there can be as Dr. Gary Sweeten says "substantial healing" in the here and now, with full healing coming in heaven when we will all be whole. With reliance on God, daily discipline, and a fellowship of "fellow travelers" on the recovery road with you, recovery can become a habit—a lifestyle of its own.

If a person is going to develop a recovery lifestyle, what principles must guide his experiences day to day? What steps must he follow in order to recover and prevent relapse?

There is a simple plan based on scriptural truth which has guided thousands of people for many years. This plan grew out of the Wesleyan Revivals of the 19th century in England. Earnest young people gathered with Charles and John Wesley to study God's word in order to find a method of spiritual growth for their lives. The plan or method that emerged later resulted in the Oxford Fellowship Principles

and provided the basis of the Twelve Steps developed by Bill
W. and the other founders of Alcoholics Anonymous.

> The Twelve Steps is not a program sponsored by any particular
> religious group or entity. Though people using this program
> find it harmonious with their own personal theology and
> spiritual beliefs, it has no official religious affiliation. It is,
> however, a program that helps us to rediscover its importance
> in our lives. We learn to live our lives according to the guidance
> of our Higher Power, God. We realize that the void or despair
> we have felt is caused by ignoring or rejecting our relationship
> with our Lord, Jesus Christ.
>
> With God's power, The Twelve Step Program becomes an
> empowering tool to relieve our suffering, fill our emptiness,
> and help us extend God's presence in our lives. This will
> release great quantities of energy, love, and joy, which we have
> never before known. It is a program that we follow at our own
> pace, in our way, with God's help and the suppport of others
> who are in the Program. All we need is an open mind and a
> willingness to try. Much of the work will be done by God
> working through us. We will suddenly notice improvements in
> ourselves: our awareness, our sensitivity, our ability to love to
> be free. We will often be surprised by our spiritual and
> emotional growth.[1]

People begin their journey of recovery in many different
ways. Some know Jesus Christ as their Savior and Lord, and
acknowledge Him as their Higher Power. Others believe in
God, and even in Jesus, but have never made a personal
commitment of faith. Still others are curious, open, and
questioning about whether God, if He does exist, cares about
them. The Twelve Steps will work for anyone, regardless of
where they are in their spiritual journey—if they are willing
to hear God's voice. Dr. Ronald R. Rand, developer of the
internationally known HELPER Clinic (How To Equip Lay
People To Evangelize Regularly), puts it this way when he
counsels inquirers: Be willing to give as much of yourself as
you know, to as much of God as you presently understand.

You see, it only takes a mustard seed of faith to begin the recovery journey. I have seen many people who start as agnostics or nominal believers who later have come to a deep faith in Christ as their Higher Power as a result of working the process of a Twelve Step Program. The classic Twelve Steps of Alcoholics Anonymous have been adapted to many other anonymous programs of recovery. In Appendix E is an adaptation of the Twelve Steps and related Scriptures reprinted from *The Twelve Steps—A Spiritual Journey*.

ATTITUDE, ATTITUDE, ATTITUDE

When a person starts down the road to recovery, what attitudes are necessary? Dr. Paul Toms, longtime pastor of Park Street Church in Boston, used to tell his congregation that the most important thing in the Christian lifestyle is "Attitude, Attitude, Attitude." I think Dr. Toms is right! In recovery, the same is true. (In reality, the path to recovery and the path to "the Christian life" are not very different!) In many ways, the steps a Christian in recovery needs to focus on are the same steps from which all of us could benefit. The differences that I have noted between recovering people and those others who are "just born again" are that the recovering people seem to take their daily walk more seriously; are less apt to hide their faults; really *do* "let go and let God" more often than not; and seem to recognize what is at stake if they do not live "one day at a time," trusting God moment by moment. (This is not to say that one cannot be mature as a Christian without a recovery program, but my guess would be that if you examine the spiritual program of someone who is truly a mature believer, you will discover the same principles at work as we see in recovery.)

What attitudes are necessary to begin the recovery process? I have noticed six.

(1) Openness to learn about, face, and deal with your *own* codependency. Many Christians (and other people) like to gain new information. They are "know it all" junkies. They climb on every new bandwagon, learn the terminology, and BANG! they think they have mastered this or that problem personally. Unfortunately, information, at least in regard to codependency, is not enough. As Dr. Gary Sweeten says: "Tellin ain't sellin!" Head knowledge in the Christian life is not enough to get you saved, and it is not enough to help you recover from codependency.

Codependent people love to be competent. They are *sure* that if they read enough books, go to enough seminars, listen to enough tapes, then their own codependency will just vanish. Sorry, it does not work that way. To begin recovery and keep recovery going, you must come to grips emotionally with your own pain. This acknowledgment is no mere intellectual assent, no mere nodding the head and shedding a few crocodile tears. It involves breaking down your denial and allowing the feelings to surface. Often a professional therapist is needed to facilitate this uncovering process. If we do not properly acknowledge and grieve our past losses they will continue to haunt us. Many people *say* they want to get out of old, sick patterns but are unwilling to *act* on their words. The emotional payoff for staying stuck in these old patterns is too strong. Perhaps they would have to stop playing victim; or get a job; or stop feeling sorry for themselves; or give up all the attention that comes from their caretaking. The payoffs are many and as various as the people who experience them. Yet to recover, all of these things must *go*. We must as John Sandford says, develop a "hatred" for our sick patterns of behavior so we are willing to give them up. If we are hanging on to these old patterns of behavior, perhaps we do not hate them enough!

(2) **Courage to focus on your own needs and the needs of others *in balance*.** This attitude is necessary because it is frightening at first to give up lifelong habits of focusing *only* on others. Many codependent people have no idea how they feel, what they need, what they like—about anything! When

they have thought of themselves, it has been in an anti-dependent manner that swings over to the other extreme in an "All or Nothing" fashion. They have never learned to be interdependent, to give and receive. Beginning to do so can be very threatening. Even *thinking* about themselves produces severe guilt and anxiety attacks for some, so it takes courage to become interdependent.

(3) **Willingness to set boundaries, limits for yourself and others.** Telling ourselves we "ought" to take time for ourselves, and actually *doing* it are two different things. I talked to a pastor today over brunch. He was planning an inner-healing retreat and because he had never done it, he wanted my input. We chatted for an hour, and at the end of the meal, he asked if I had any closing thoughts to help him prepare. I told him that for me it is always essential to plan time prior and after such an all-day event for prayer and rest, otherwise Satan tended to use my weariness to discourage and defeat me. He looked sheepish and replied, "I know I should, but I am booked up to the middle of June! [It's early April now!] I don't have any days or evenings off!" Later we prayed together that he would have God's wisdom as to what needed to be cut from his schedule.

You must be willing to set limits for yourself as well as for inappropriate behaviors and behaviors of others who make inappropriate demands. There must also be a willingness to reset boundaries around receiving from others! It's odd to me how codependent people can think that no boundaries are needed regarding *their* giving, but they set up brick walls whenever others try to give to them! They feel guilty when they do not give, and guilty when they receive. In recovery, they learn to have a balance between giving and receiving.

(4) **Recognition of and patience with the healing process involved in recovery.** Ever sprain your ankle and try to rush the healing? You think, *I don't need those crutches! They're for weaklings!* and Boom! Next thing you know you are "flat on your fanny" with an even worse sprain than before. Or, as

116

a kid, did you ever pick at a scab or pimple until it got infected? You thought you would hurry it along by picking at it and Voilá! More problems!

So it is with recovery from codependency or other addictions. There is a process involved, and those who have been down the path before warn that you cannot fly ahead and skip any steps. I had a client who was a new Christian, a recovering alcoholic (one year sober), and a newly acknowledged Adult Child of Alcoholism. He was one of those people who remind you of a computer. He could say the right things, but "the voice" seemed mechanical and without emotion. He was terrified of getting in touch with his real emotions. He grabbed his Twelve Step workbook and began to whip right through to step four. (Step four involves making a fearless and searching moral inventory of your life.) All of a sudden he was stuck. I knew it was coming but decided to let him find out on his own. He realized that he had been intellectualizing his step-work and his therapy, and was unwilling to face the feelings lurking under his depression. Since then, he has gotten honest with a group of recovering men with whom he meets regularly, and he is doing much better.

Recovery involves a process, and you must be willing to let God take you through it in His way—not yours. (See—even in recovery, codependents try to control!) Isaiah 55:8 says that God's ways are not our ways, and in recovery that is especially true. Jeremiah 17:9 says that our heart is "deceitful" and "desperately sick" (NASV) and that we cannot, on our own, know or understand ourselves fully. Verse 10 says that *the Lord* is the one who searches the hearts and tests the minds. So who are we to tell God how fast or slow our recovery should progress? There is a tendency to want to run ahead of the Lord, thinking we know best. Sitting still and waiting for His timing is not easy, but it is necessary.

(5) Openness to a deeper spiritual life. As was mentioned earlier, the principles in a recovery program, if the program is designed properly, will enhance and facilitate personal growth—including spiritual growth. In fact, historically, as I said earlier, the Twelve Steps, used as a basis for AA and other step-group approaches, come out of the Wesleyan revivals in England during the nineteenth century. Wesley and his colleagues developed a "method" to grow spiritually (hence "Methodism") and the basis of these methods became, years later, the Twelve Steps.

Openness to God and searching your heart is crucial. We can mouth the words but really being open is another matter. Psalm 139:23 is an especially helpful prayer for those in recovery. We all need to be open to God, but when someone has lived in denial for a long time, there is a special need.

For many of us, denial has been a major tool for survival. Denial is a learned pattern of behavior, and as such, is incredibly cunning. We can consciously deny reality by telling a blatant lie to hide some truth about ourselves or someone else. Conversely, we can be unaware of our denial by the secrets we keep from ourselves. Denial can block any and all reality from our minds. It cleverly protects us from realizing the consequences of our actions, because we simply do not acknowledge or accept responsibility for them. The power of denial is represented biblically by Peter in his denial of Christ. It was less painful for Peter to deny that he was a follower of Christ than to face the consequences of admitting his relationship with Him. Peter's fear of recrimination and rebuke was stronger than his love for Jesus. In a similar way, we prefer to continue behavior that "saves face," rather than to acknowledge reality and accept the consequences of our actions. We find it easier to hide from our true feelings by being seemingly overattentive to our families, our churches, and our jobs. Staying busy allows us to ignore true feelings, thereby denying them.

Openness to a new view of God as Father is also a prerequisite to recovery. As we discussed earlier, we humans tend to see God the Father through all our perceptions of our earthly fathers. Thus, we end up worshiping a "false" god rather than the scriptural God. Note I said "openness to a new view"—not that we must "have" a new view with which to start. Part of the process is acquiring an accurate view of God so that we can run to Him as "Abba" (Daddy) rather than viewing Him as we do our earthly fathers. But many people have seen God negatively for so long, and they are not quite open to letting go of that image. And so, unfortunately, they are not quite ready to recover.

The new, deeper spiritual life will also have the added dimension of gratitude. Many codependent people have been bitter, hurt, sad, and depressed for so long that they have quite forgotten how to be grateful, if they ever knew in the first place. The kind of gratitude codependent people know about, prior to recovery, is the kind a person feels when someone stops beating their head against the wall. Real, genuine gratitude, biblical rejoicing (Phil. 4:4), is something they do not understand. Usually, in their view, there has been little for which to be grateful! So there needs to be an openness to changing one's views on life and openness to cultivating gratitude, even if the person doesn't *feel* grateful yet. Most codependents feel, deep down, that God *owes* them one, or two or three, so developing a new attitude of openness is sometimes difficult, but again, necessary.

(6) Willingness to get help and support. Codependents are great at helping others, but they find it extremely painful to ask for help themselves. They are eager to tell others what is wrong and how to get better, but find it distasteful to have to admit needing help themselves. Doctors, ministers, and other helping professionals are some of the most difficult people in treatment, because they are always looking at the other guy rather than themselves. Yet, even ordinary codependent people need help. No one can recover on his own! It is tempting to read a few books, listen to a few tapes, and try to work the Twelve Steps alone, using a workbook. Tapes and books and workbooks are great, but they will not be an adequate substitute for other human beings. Going it alone is dangerous because it perpetuates the secret and thus the shame around one's codependency. Shame disappears and the secrets lose their power when confession is put into regular practice! James 5:16 means what it says: There is healing when we confess to one another and pray for one another. Elijah (the Old Testament prophet) learned the hard way that going it alone only produces burnout. It made him forget all the other believers in Yahweh out there (1 Kings 19). We need one another and it is important to let go of self-pride and admit it.

SEEKING HELP

Treatment versus Therapy

Some people use the terms "therapy" and "treatment" synonymously; I do not. In my view, "treatment" consists of those steps necessary to help a person begin a recovery program. "Therapy" consists of those steps necessary to deal with the more all-encompassing root problems in a person's emotional and spiritual life.[3] Treatment sets people on the road to recovery. It gets them "sober," if you will. It enables them to stop the compulsive acting-in/acting-out cycle of their addictive behaviors. When people are still "medicating" their feelings by acting out with their substance or experience, it will be impossible to do therapy. Their energy and emotions are tied up in the addictive process and are not "available" for therapy. Until recovery is begun, therapy (looking at deeper issues) is pointless, much as it is pointless with someone who is an alcoholic, yet refuses to stop drinking while seeking therapy. This is not to say people should not seek help until recovery is begun, but rather to realize that, at first, the "help" will focus on recovery not therapy *per se*. When people are codependent, especially when they are addicted to a specific relationship, they will remain obsessed with changing or fixing the other person and/or themselves so "they will love me," until the cycle of addiction is broken. While trapped in codependent patterns, people are not able to look beyond the pain of the moment to the deeper root causes. The first step is to focus on breaking the addictive cycle of codependency.[4]

While this is an important principle, there are exceptions and overlapping circumstances. For example, sometimes when working with incest victims who have an eating disorder, I find that their eating patterns (their actions and behavior) are directly linked to the incest trauma. In this type of situation a therapist may need to work with some of the deeper therapy issues, while they still help the person stop the compulsive behaviors. Yet, obviously when a person is an incest survivor, if their eating disorder is life-threatening, it must be treated *before* any deeper traumas can be addressed. It would be impossible for a dead client to work on any kind of trauma!

Goals for Treatment

There are a number of goals during the treatment phase. Once again, the most important goal is to stop the acting-out behavior. This step includes setting limits on self-destructive behaviors by the person and by others. A person needs to have support and guidance to achieve this goal. Some people begin this process with a sponsor[5] from a support group; others, with a pastor who understands codependency; still others, with a professional therapist trained in this area. The point is that to stop acting out (engaging in the compulsive codependent behaviors), the person needs support. Gritting one's teeth and swearing to stop will not work. Help must be sought outside the self.

Another goal is for the person to understand how unmanageable their life has become because of their codependent behaviors and how powerless they are to change it. This understanding is not a mere intellectual understanding, as was mentioned earlier. There must be a "coming to grips" with the emotional losses, the helplessness, the compulsiveness of the disorder. Treatment also has the goal of providing the atmosphere where the client can understand exactly what his own compulsive codependent patterns are like, in a primary relationship and in other areas of life. Along with the understanding comes the goal of gaining insight into what underlying emotions are being "medicated" or avoided because of acting codependently. The person will also confront shame and self-blame during treatment and face the effects these two feelings have had in his life.

During treatment, some new steps will be taken, which include:

(1) working toward new self-definition by taking responsibility for himself in every area of life;

(2) coming to a deeper commitment to God through Jesus Christ, as *the* source of restoration and sanity, and hence a decision to turn over his will and life to God;

(3) engaging in a "fearless moral inventory" (step four in a twelve-step program), honestly examining behavior, thoughts, beliefs, and feelings in every area of life;

(4) learning how to set appropriate boundaries so as to reduce shame when in abusive social or family settings;

(5) learning to accept personal needs as a valid part of a balanced life of giving *and* receiving;

(6) learning to receive appropriately as well as to give (this includes learning to receive nurture from himself as well as others);

(7) gaining intimacy skills and the ability to maintain close, meaningful relationships in family and support networks;

(8) developing a clear plan for lifelong recovery, including therapy, lifestyle changes, career development, and relapse prevention.

Figure 8

DEPENDENCY SCALE

DEPENDENT	INTERDEPENDENT	ANTI-DEPENDENT
NEEDY MARTYR/VICTIM CONTROLLER PASSIVE LOW SELF ESTEEM ANXIETY HIGHS/LOWS COMPULSIVE OVERLY RESPONSIBLE	INTIMACY CLOSENESS AFFECTION MUTUALITY GIVE AND TAKE COMPANIONSHIP SERENITY	"I'M A ROCK, AN ISLAND" USUALLY A WORKOHOLIC "I DON'T NEED ANYBODY" LOW SELF-ESTEEM MASKED BY: • BRAVADO • EMOTIONAL HIGHS AND LOWS • DRIVENNESS

©1989 Margaret J. Rinck

Goals for Therapy

Once a person has stopped acting out, and is well on the road to recovery, his energy is no longer directed toward the addictive behavior(s). Now he is ready to go deeper into the problem, and "therapy" begins. The therapy phase is somewhat less structured than the treatment phase, but is still oriented toward skill development. The focus will be mostly on family of origin issues, relational issues, inner healing, and emotional work.

The goals of therapy include the following:

(1) maintaining a lifestyle free of codependent acting out;

(2) growth in interdependence (see figure 8);

(3) learning new coping skills;

(4) growth in Christian maturity/community/fellowship;

(5) resolution of abuse issues and other family of origin work;

(6) completing of the first journey through the Twelve Steps.

ASPECTS OF ADDICTION

Any *treatment* program, whether in a self-help group or in a professional setting, must address particular aspects of the addictive behavior.[6] These aspects are preoccupation, rituals, behaviors, unmanageability, emotions, and thinking. When seeking help, a person needs to be sure that each of these following areas are part of the program.

There are also certain questions that are important for a recovering person to ask himself regarding each aspect of the addictive behavior. Any treatment program chosen also needs to address these questions. The following are the types of questions any recovering person should deal with carefully.

Preoccupation. What is your addictive cycle? What happens that hooks you into acting-out codependently? What happens that hooks you into acting in—trying not to do your compulsive, codependent "things" but feeling just as compulsive as ever? How long does a typical codependent cycle of interaction last? How does it end? What do you do to stay focused on your addictive behavior after the interaction? What stops the preoccupation? How long until it starts again? With what thoughts, feelings, behaviors are you preoccupied?

Rituals. What rituals (ritualized, repetitive behaviors, actions) do you use to maintain the codependency?

Behaviors. What behaviors do you engage in when acting out your codependency? Patterns? Types of behavior? Extent? When trying to control your codependency ("acting in")? What triggers set you off to react codependently? How much time do you spend on each behavior?

Unmanageability. What behaviors on your part have gone out of control? What losses have you experienced because of your codependent relationships? How has your codependency affected your life? Your finances? How much time have you lost focusing on changing your husband or wife or child (or wishing they'd change)? What toll has your codependency taken on your health? Your emotions? Your spiritual life? What other compulsive behaviors have developed in your life?

Emotions. What underlying emotions are you "medicating" by remaining codependent? What is your level of depression? Anxiety? Are you suicidal? Do you have manic episodes?

Thinking. Are you demonstrating any psychotic thought patterns? Paranoia? (Psychotic thought patterns would include hallucinations, delusions, hearing voices, confused thinking and speech. Paranoia means thinking that people or a group is against you or out to harm you or make you a special object of attention.) What rationalizations do you use to maintain the addiction to your person or experience? What are your core addictive beliefs? In what ways is your thinking distorted? What defense mechanisms do you use? In what way are you in denial? What are the catalytic events or environments that have shaped your beliefs?

The reason these questions are important is that people just entering treatment have a lot of denial. Focusing on these questions helps break down the denial. In each phase of treatment there is certain content to be covered. It can also be summarized using the above six categories, as follows:

Preoccupation. Here the therapist teaches the person the role preoccupation plays in maintaining codependency. The concept of the "addictive personality shift" is introduced.[7] This concept is helpful because it allows people to distance themselves from "the part of them" which is codependent. They can label it their "addict" or their "codependent" self, or whatever term helps them detach from themselves a bit. We teach clients that when they are tempted to act out to remember that their personality is shifting gears and that they are starting to listen to their "addict" again. People in the AA Twelve Step programs use this concept when they say "That's just my disease talking." This technique helps the person realize that they have a choice and can say no to the old patterns.

When working with preoccupation, we help people grieve the "loss" of their addictive relationships. Robin Norwood says that codependents, to some extent, become "addicted to excitement."[8] They actually begin to miss the chaos, so we teach them to let go of it and grieve the loss. Many codependents have never known anything but chaos interpersonally, so this change is quite traumatic.

We also begin to teach them new coping mechanisms to deal with their anxiety. In the past, they used codependent behaviors to stifle their fears. Now they need new methods, such as meditation on Scripture, journal writing, and relaxation exercises. The next step is to help the client become aware of their personal limits and vulnerabilities. No matter how weak they feel, codependents invariably demand too much of themselves. They are rigidly perfectionistic and have a difficult time accepting their personal fallibility without irrational self-blame.

Rituals. First we place an injunction on rituals. Then we replace their old rituals with new ones. For example, in the past the person may have bought cards and gifts for the person with whom he was obsessed whenever he felt insecure. Now we encourage them to find a sponsor or a mentor and encourage such practices as the Twelve Step meetings; use of journals to record their thoughts and feelings; and use of workbooks for personal growth. Next we set up a date for stopping behaviors. The step after that is to recognize progress regularly by celebrating their progress symbolically, for example, by means of self-rewards, group celebration, or group recognition.

Behaviors. Here we contract with the person regarding limits on his codependent behaviors. We also provide training in new coping behavior and assist them in establishing codependent "sobriety." For example, Matthew's estranged wife has asked him for a six-week "time-out" contract between them. During this period they agree not to have any contact whatsoever with one another. Yet Matthew has still called Lynn every day for the past two weeks, whenever he has felt lonely or sad about their relationship. Contracting with him regarding this codependent behavior would require that Matthew make a commitment to his therapist or sponsor that he will not call Lynn, but instead that he will call a support person. Thus, he receives the support he needs when he's feeling lonely, and he still respects the "time-out" contract that he made with his wife.

Unmanageability. At this stage, we use the unmanageability they have discovered as a lever to contract for change. We initiate second-order change to disrupt the system. "First order change" is whatever unsuccessful strategy a person repeatedly uses to try to change their own or someone else's behavior. Despite the lack of success of their "first-order" change strategy, the individual keeps repeating their strategy over and over. For example, Marvin knows that it is futile to try to nag Catherine, his anorectic wife, to eat. Even so, he nags her on a regular basis. She gets angry and resents his controlling behavior. She retaliates against Marvin by eating even less. And so, their little cycle repeats itself endlessly. A "second-order change" would be a change that disrupts the typical functioning of the system that operates between Marvin and Catherine. This disruption is usually something paradoxical or different. For example, instead of nagging Catherine, Marvin might choose to ignore her eating habits. Marvin decides to fix his own meals and begins to attend a support group for friends and family members of persons with eating disorders. Marvin has shifted the focus to himself. He's made the decision to work on what he can change in their relationship (himself) rather than on what he cannot change (Catherine and her eating habits). Catherine no longer has a reason to resent Marvin, and she no longer needs to retaliate. Consider that Jesus frequently used paradoxes in His teaching. One paradox that is particularly helpful for recovering people is His principle of "losing your life in order to gain it." First-order thinking involves seeking one's own life to gain it, whereas Jesus taught that one should lose their life in order to gain it (second-order thinking). Sometimes we have to admit that we are "powerless" and that our lives are "unmanageable." We must lose our illusion of control and personal competence before we are once again empowered and can live successful, meaningful lives.

Helping the person to be honest about feelings and thinking, we reinforce Step 1 (regarding unmanageability) when denial creeps in again. And we help them to accept their human imperfections and need for help from others (Step 4). We guide them through Steps 2 and 3 (regarding accepting help from God) and we help them learn how to assess their susceptibility to relapse.

Emotions. When in treatment, a person will experience many new emotions. They are stopping their acting-out/acting-in cycle of compulsive behaviors, which in the past prevented their actual feelings from emerging. Often this reemergence of feelings will be quite intense and painful. Sometimes a physician and/or psychiatrist will need to be consulted about possible medication and/or hospitalization, due to severe depression. We teach the clients to understand how their thoughts, beliefs, and "self-talk" produce their feelings and emotions.[9] We also help them develop criteria by which to evaluate their habitual thinking and beliefs. We also teach the role of shame and guilt in recovery and establish relapse prevention strategies.

Here a person needs to arrange for appropriate medications from their doctor, if necessary, to manage depression. Hospitalization is sometimes necessary due to the severity of depression. We teach the ABC's of emotion and the Five Rules of Rational Thinking and Feeling. We also teach the role of shame and guilt in recovery and establish relapse prevention strategies.

Thinking. Here we confront gross defenses and work to help people accept the situation. We encourage them to confront impatient or distorted thinking. We also teach feedback mechanisms to help them keep reality in focus, and we assign them a task (e.g., write out a "secrets" list) to help deal with the shame they carry.

The process that we have outlined here is not necessarily done in this order. There may be overlap. The essential point is that care is taken to address all of these areas.

Once *treatment* has addressed the above-mentioned aspects of addiction (preoccupation, rituals, behaviors, unmanageability, emotions, and thinking), *therapy* issues can be addressed. There are additional aspects of addictive behavior which must be addressed therapeutically. For example, addicted people have lost years of their lives, relationships with friends and family, money, self-esteem, jobs/careers, educational opportunities, etc., all because of their compulsive behaviors. There is also much personal emotional trauma due to their addiction, which must be addressed.

The goal of therapy is for people to review their lives and

FIGURE 9

HEALING SHAME AND FEAR OF ABANDONMENT

INNER (INSIDE YOURSELF)	OUTER (OUTSIDE IN THE WORLD)
Decide to give up shaming yourself. Commit to uncovering your secrets. Renounce patterns of self-blame.	Talk about the secrets (Break the No-Talk Rule). - Secret Shame List - Confession Principle - 12 Step Group - Sponsor - Pastor, Therapist
Renew your mind. Change your thoughts regarding: - Self - Others - God - Situations	Act Assertively. - Act, don't react - Know what you think and feel - "Say - Ask" Formula (say what you need first, then ask your question)
Come alive, develop awareness, refuse to merely "go through the motions".	Notice your body (How does it look, feel, smell, talk, sit?). Notice your feelings and thoughts. Be alert for positive things around you; list fifteen positive items a day. Pay attention to the environment, keep a journal and record what you notice.
Decide to accept yourself as you are. Reject driving yourself to be perfect. Give yourself permission to be human. Forgive yourself for failures.	Act lovingly toward yourself by - Disciplining yourself - Delaying gratification appropriately - Resting, relaxing, having fun - Meeting your needs in healthy ways - Developing a balanced lifestyle - Parenting yourself
Commit to always "being there" for your inner child.	Get a photo of yourself when you were less than five years old. Frame and place it where you will see it often. Talk regularly to the child and reassure him that you "are there" for him.
Set your will to protect yourself, help yourself love, forgive, and accept yourself in healthy ways.	Use thought-stopping, new self-talk, and healthy distraction techniques to reprogram old patterns of self-hate, unforgiveness, rejection of self.
Determine to strengthen your ability to use the support resources that are available to you, within and without yourself. Commit to Jesus Christ as your "Ultimate Support Person."	List your resources on paper. Example: God's Word, church, best friend, sibling, Jesus, gifts and fruit of Holy Spirit, prayer, meditation, fasting, singing, counseling, school, work, career guidance, relatives, friends, small groups, etc.

their relationships systematically to rebuild them and reclaim lost parts of their lives. Many losses have occurred in their lives with which they have yet to come to grips. Thus, family-of-origin work is crucial.

During this part of the recovery process, people examine their own contributions to the problems and their family of origin's influence. They examine these areas, not to heap blame or shame on themselves or others, but rather to face the pain, and forgive others and themselves. It is quite important to have a therapist who understands this process and is skilled in integrating Christian principles into their work.

Another area of importance in the therapy phase is the healing of the roots of addiction: shame and fear of abandonment. While no one will ever be perfectly healed of every hurt or problem until the Lord comes again, or we die and go to heaven, there can be substantial healing now. God's power and promises are still available to us today. Thus, Christian therapy has as a goal the inner healing of the individual both psychologically and spiritually. In my forthcoming book on misogyny (hatred of women) (*Christian Men Who Hate Women*, Zondervan 1990)[10] I use the chart in figure 9 to explain the various steps to be taken in healing shame and fear of abandonment. These steps are not necessarily in any particular order, nor do the "inner" steps come prior to the "outer" steps. Each person is different, and a therapist or pastor must be sensitive in guiding the person through these steps. This chart can be used as a checklist to monitor progress in therapy.

THE HEALING PROCESS

Healing the underlying shame and fear of abandonment is fundamental to the recovery process. Each person must, in a sense, go through a reparenting process. Usually a therapist or sponsor acts as a guide or mentor for this crucial process. This type of inner work demands from the recovering person a number of growth steps. Four growth steps will enable the healing to take place. (We are distinguishing these *steps* from the recovery program Twelve Steps.)

Be Honest

The first step involves **unremitting honesty.** Our tendency as human beings is to want to see what is wrong with the other person, not what is wrong with us. Codependent people, because of their extreme tendency to focus on the other person, often have a hard time making the shift to self-examination. Often they have been taken advantage of, abused, neglected, or unappreciated. So they naturally feel hurt or angry. It is easy for them to shift into the victim position, and because there has been legitimate suffering on their part, they resist shifting the focus to *their* behaviors. Also, they need a willingness to be honest about how codependency has affected other relationships beyond their male-female relationships. Some people are willing to admit being codependent with their spouses or dating partners, but are reluctant to "see" how codependently they act with their boss, their mom and dad, their children, and same-sex relationships. This type of honesty takes courage because it means reassessing their entire lifestyle developed over many years. Sometimes shame and embarrassment keep them from noticing that their codependency is as pervasive as it really is. One woman recently told me how surprised she was to notice that even with other women, she based the relationship entirely on caretaking. She said that it seemed to her that "if I was not either giving (caretaking) or being cared *for*, there was *nothing* to bind us together." Caretaking or being the object of caretaking was the only way she knew how to relate to other people. For some codependent people, being as honest as this woman was is difficult at first.

Recognize the Little Child Within

The second growth step necessary for the recovering person to possess is the **courage to acknowledge, listen to, and love the little child within himself.** Whenever a person comes from a dysfunctional family, and did not receive what he needed as a little child, for whatever reason, it is as if there was part of him that stopped growing. He became frozen in time, stuck at two or three or five years old, whenever the pain became too much to bear. Normally the childlike part of us gets integrated into a stable whole personality. However, for these people, the child is either a forgotten figure, lost in the chaos of early life, or is an overgrown brat who wants to sabotage anything the adult person wants to accomplish. Some people find that their inner child, as we call this part of ourselves, flips between these two extremes—one minute the abused, pathetic, hurting victim; the next, the bully who tries to dominate everything. Instead of becoming childlike, these people have become childish. Some codependent people have been keenly aware of their own inner child, and associate it with all that is weak, despised, bad, and worthless. They hate the self that was once a child. Others are not even aware of one side or the other (the victim or the bully). Not having been parented in such a way as to learn how to integrate their childlike qualities into loving adult behavior, and how to discipline the childish parts of self without violence or self-hatred, these people need courage to face this inner child and to learn reparenting skills.

Forgive

The third growth step is a **willingness to face the pain from the past and forgive those people who have hurt them.** While only God can forgive perfectly, forgiveness remains the foundation stone to all healing. Without it, little can be accomplished. Many codependent people begin recovery with an unforgiving attitude. As they progress, learn grati-

133

tude, and see their own brokenness and selfishness, forgiveness becomes easier.

It is beyond the scope of this book to go into detail on this subject. There are many excellent books and tapes available which will enable you to grow into the ability to forgive. Forgiveness is a process. We can set our will to forgive and trust God to slowly bring our feelings of hurt, anger, and pain in line. Facing the feelings is a vital first step. If I have only faced half of the pain in my heart, I can only forgive someone for half of the pain. Many times a professional therapist becomes a valuable helper in digging into the past to release the pain. We cannot bring the hurt to Jesus for healing if we do not let ourselves feel it! (See the resource list in Appendix C for books on forgiveness.)

Complete a Recovery Plan

The fourth growth step necessary to recovery is the **discipline to develop and carry out a recovery plan**. Recovering people need to have a clear focus of their goals for one month, three months, six months, twelve months. When people do not aim at the target, they will not hit it! Along with broad goals, a recovery plan needs to have a list of names of people who are supportive and who understand recovery, a relapse prevention guide, and a plan of what to do if a relapse does occur. See Appendix A for a sample plan.

The following case study illustrates the end result of one young woman's struggle with these four growth steps needed for her recovery plan. The letter she wrote to her father was not actually sent to him, but was written as her way of actively expressing her forgiveness. It took this young woman almost one year of therapy to be able to write this letter.

Sandi is a young woman in her mid-thirties. A businesswoman, Sandi is bright, attractive, energetic, well-liked, and successful. Outwardly she looks like she has everything. For many years, however, Sandi suffered from undiagnosed

134

depression. A chronic caretaker like her mom, she tried as the eldest child to caretake her six younger siblings and mediate the conflicts between her father and her mother.

Her father is a multi-millionaire, a womanizer (probably a sexual addict), and an active alcoholic. Her mother is codependent and tends to exaggerate to the point of lying. She has been divorced from her husband for two to three years.

Sandi was raised in a religious home and came to a personal relationship with Christ in her early twenties. Sandi's mother became involved in a renewal movement and developed a personal relationship with Jesus. This spiritual awakening led her out of her codependent denial sufficiently that she was able to recognize that her husband was leading a double life. She hired a detective who discovered that he had an apartment and a condo and another woman. At the time, Sandi was twenty-three years old. She left her job out of state to come home and "care" for Mom. More and more, the facts of her father's double life came to light. For months, Sandi devoted herself to caring for Mom, who was severely depressed. Sandi did not grieve at all herself. She took a menial job, cared for Mom, and slept thirteen hours a day. She saw a psychologist briefly. Her dad "lived at home more or less" until one winter he "officially" moved out. He promptly had a heart attack. One brother moved in with Dad to help him but got sick and had to move out. Sandi felt guilty, but she did not speak to her father for nearly one year.

Over the next ten years, Sandi's father would repeat a pattern of reconciling with her mother, moving back in, then seeing other women again, and finally moved back out. Two years ago, the primary woman (#1) he had been seeing was "born again" and refused to sleep with him. He left her and lived with woman #2 for six months. Then a few months later, he decided to move out of #2's condo; #2 became angry, so he broke up with her and bought another condo. He began reading the Bible, bought a huge house, and announced his plans to marry woman #1.

135

At this point, Sandi, woman #1, and Sandi's siblings arranged an intervention, hoping to persuade him to seek alcoholism treatment. He denied that he had a problem and became very angry with the group. Woman #1 told Sandi, "I will handle him."

During her twenties and thirties, Sandi had a series of destructive relationships with men. We uncovered in therapy a repetition compulsion (a tendency to repeat destructive patterns in relationships despite their negative consequences) stemming from her relationship with her dad. There has also been incest among her siblings. Sandi suspects that she herself was molested by her father. Due to one of these unhealthy liaisons with other men, Sandi got pregnant. She wanted to keep the baby. Her friends at church were not supportive, but her mother and sister were. She lost the child midterm and was unable to acknowledge her grief and pain at the time.

Until recently, Sandi had maintained a business relationship with her father. He tended to use money to manipulate and control the family. She understood this and she had taken steps to break any financial ties with him. She has been angry with him because he was never there for her emotionally and used dollars as a way to "buy" her love.

Sandi is presently dating a fine Christian man. She is growing and becoming healthier due to intensive therapy and a seven-week stay at a Christian psychiatry facility. She entered the hospital treatment program because, as her dad approached his third marriage, she became more and more despondent. She had two to three episodes of self-destructive behavior. She began crying, screaming, and hitting herself or hitting her head against the furniture. On one occasion she hit her boyfriend when she became angry because he did not understand her feelings.

While in the hospital program, Sandi wrote the following "letter" to her dad. She did not intend to send it, but wrote it for her own growth. She gave me permission to share it. It is an example of how important expressing feelings is, and how much forgiveness is part of the process of healing.

Dear Dad—

I am writing this letter to you—and it is truly unbelievable to me, but I am not angry with you (anymore). God has done a marvelous thing in me. He has brought me to a place where I chose to forgive you! It is unbelievable to me. But I do forgive you—even feel love for you. I love you, Dad. You are my dad. God gave you to me to be my dad. You have not been the dad I've wanted. I wanted a dad who would spend time with me. I wanted a dad who would genuinely encourage me in my goals. Dad, you're a good businessman. I wanted your instruction on how to be a good businesswoman. I wanted your help, Dad— Dad, I wanted you to be proud and satisfied in the things I accomplished in my life, and I wanted you to tell me how proud you are of me. I wanted to know, Dad, how much you loved me—I wanted to know, Dad, that you loved me. Mostly, I wanted your time, your ear, your wisdom, your love, your encouragement, your counsel, your good fatherly affection. I wanted to be treated by you, Dad, the way you would want my husband to treat me.

I wanted to know that you knew you had faults, too, and weren't perfect. And I wanted to know that you knew you could make mistakes, too, Dad. I wanted to hear you say "I'm sorry" for the things you did that really hurt me and that were wrong. I wish you'd have done that, Dad. I wish you'd have helped me see that it was not my beauty, my body, and my little girl performance that would "get" me a man, but rather that it is my sincere heart, my listening to God, my using my intellect, my giving to others from a no-expectation place. Yes, my keeping up with my hair, face, and body, but that was not the most important thing. That what lives inside of me is the most important thing.

I love you, Dad. I wish you were these things for me. It would have made my growing up into womanhood easier to know you supported me in who I was and am.

But you didn't. And now I am learning about these things. I need to know these things, Dad, because I desire to be a good woman for the man God has chosen for me.

I wish—I wish—I could say that forever, Dad, but, now, I realize I can stop wishing and wanting and desiring and hoping you'll change, Dad, because Dad, I decided to change. I no longer am that raging, fuming, angry daughter, a person whose needs were, I felt, never met. I have and I am giving that up, Dad. I am choosing to forgive you. I forgive you.

I chose last Tuesday, 7 March and had to again on Wednesday 8 March—and I might have to again and again. But I choose to forgive you. Let me tell you what happened inside of me when I chose to forgive you.

First, nothing. Absolutely nothing. And then I was so angry at God because I thought God had failed me, too! But this man at the hospital set me straight and let me know that I may not feel anything and that forgiveness was an act of the will, not a feeling. I didn't like hearing that. I wanted to feel I had forgiven you. (It was hard, too, Dad, to come to a place where I was going to choose to forgive you because I wanted you to pay for all the hurt I felt for my brothers and sisters and mom. You must pay for what I felt.)

Secondly, I realized I took back the forgiveness I gave you the first time. I took it back from God because, like I said, I felt you had to pay. Well, then I came to realize, Dad, that I was the one paying, not you. I was the one paying—like a catch 22. If I forgave you, then it was like I was letting you off the hook, but also if I forgave you, "I'd be let off the hook."

By not forgiving you, Dad, I was destroying me. I was not able to function in a one-to-one relationship with a man because I felt that they were going to do to me what I felt you did to me. And so I always had my defenses. I would not trust anyone to let my guard down. And in business relationships there was always this mistrust and feeling like I was going to be taken advantage of—I had to stay on top, keep even with the family lifestyle.

So, I was and have been paying dearly for not forgiving you, and it finally came down to (1) me continuing to pay for not forgiving you and destroying my life, my body, my health (but at least thinking I was making you pay), or (2) forgiving you and getting on with my life and putting my thinking in order.

I decided to forgive you because it wasn't fun making you pay because you weren't paying for it—you have just kept on living the way you wanted, but I, I have been in bondage, destroying my life and anything good or alive around me.

And I *want* a relationship with a man. I can't have that—a healthy relationship—when I am in destructive bondage.

I forgave you again. But this time I didn't take it back.

Let me tell you what happened that evening after I finally realized what I was doing by forgiving you. I started to work on my collage of present pain. All of a sudden, it was like, I could continue working on it; it was like I was getting past it; I was looking at it objectively. The pain was beginning to subside!

The next day I felt encouraged and energized for the first time—first time in a long, long, long time.

And the collage, Dad. I look at the collage of all that pain and it's like yes—yes I did feel that way, but I don't feel that way now.

Dad! I have released you; I have let go, which brings me to my next point—money and you. Dad, I have always thought that if I failed, Dad will be there. He'll pick me up. He'll take care of my financial failure. He will be there. And Dad, you did for a long time while I had the shop on 10th Street and before that in college and even when I didn't ask you for anything during those years between college and the shop—it was still, well, I *can* fall back on Dad; he's there just in case. Dad, I realize now that my trust should be in God, my heavenly Father, not in you. I found my security in you but I really never knew if it would really be there, and when it was, I had to play your games and be what you wanted me to be at the sacrifice of the real me. It cost me dearly and the security was false security because it was like the guillotine every time I'd ask myself, *Well, is he or isn't he going to cut me off?* or *Is he or isn't he going to chop my self-esteem into little pieces for asking?* or *Well, is he or isn't he going to take care of me?*

Dad, I had my security in a broken cistern (Jer. 2:13) that I built myself. But God, my heavenly Father, I am realizing, is my true security whom I can faithfully rely on. He is the One who will provide me springs of living water.

Why I am saying all this, Dad, is that I realize I was wrong in depending on you to meet my financial needs. I *need* now to break from that completely, too. I do break from that completely, Dad.

Thanks for all you have done for me.

Love, Sandi

SEEKING HELP

As was mentioned before, no one can recover alone. Seeking help is difficult, but necessary. Just today a young religious worker who is an incest victim looked at me plaintively when I suggested she needed to be in an incest therapy group. She asked, "You're sure there is not any other way?" I assured her that this group was necessary for her. She nodded and grinned sheepishly. "Just thought I'd ask" seemed to be her nonverbal reply.

You are not alone if you feel awkward and embarrassed or ashamed. Codependent people feel that way whenever they have to receive anything without being able to give it back. To be on the receiving end of treatment/therapy feels "real out of control." It is normal to feel this way at first. Do not let these feelings stop you. Get help anyway.

Some people object, "But there are no Christian therapists around here!" That may or may not be true. Check the referral list in Appendix B. You may not be aware of some fine resources in your area. Others say, "But I could never go to a counselor around here. I am too well known." Confidentiality is the hallmark of professional therapy, but if you are still concerned, look for a professional therapist in a town an hour or so away from you. I have had people travel from one to three hours to see me! Therapists understand your concerns and may even be able to help you find someone closer to home, yet far enough away to preserve your privacy.

"But I am so ashamed. How could I tell a stranger all these stupid things that I have done?" Believe me, therapists are human too, and have done stupid things themselves. Also there is little that a therapist has not heard at one time or another. You may feel as if your story is too unique, bizarre, or sinful, but you may be sure that your therapist may have heard it before! And if he hasn't, he'll refer you to someone else who has experience with your problem.

"But I can't afford therapy!" Let me ask you these questions: Is your emotional/spiritual/mental/physical health worth the cost of two TV sets and a VCR? If your child needed therapy, would you find a way somehow? Why are you worth less than they are? Also, for those who have low income, all public and some private mental health agencies offer some form of a "sliding scale" where you pay only what you can afford. Many people find that their health insurance covers fifty to ninety percent of their fee for therapy. Most professional therapists are open to doing some "pro-bono" work (i.e., work for which they do not charge). Some churches also give scholarships for people who legitimately cannot afford therapy; other churches have professional therapists on their staff and offer free services to church members and/or people from the community. And the Salvation Army and other groups like Women Helping Women offer special types of counseling at little or no cost to you.

"I don't know what to look for in a therapist." There are certain things you will want to look for in a therapist, Christian or not. Ask them if they:

(1) understand and are trained in codependency work.

(2) understand and are trained in addiction recovery.

(3) are certified and licensed by your state.

(4) have cognitive-oriented style of therapy. (You want someone who will be more than just empathic and warm. You need a cognitive-skills oriented therapist who also

141

knows how to help you work through strong feelings. A cognitive-oriented therapist teaches clients how to deal with the thinking patterns that cause the unproductive or hurtful emotions. Cognitions are thoughts. These therapists teach *skills* to the client on how to think and feel differently.)

(5) are open to referring you to group therapy, workshops, or other resources if necessary.

(6) work with "inner child and grief/loss issues." What is their approach? (You want someone who can facilitate the release of long pent-up feelings as well as teach you new skills.)

(7) have a working relationship with a psychiatrist or medical doctor should medications be necessary.

(8) will tell you what methods they use in therapy.

After the first session ask yourself the following questions:

(1) **How did I like the therapist?** Do I need another session or two to really decide if I will "hit it off" with the therapist, or do I need to find someone else? If you had any questions that went unanswered, be sure to bring them up at the next visit. The patient-therapist relationship is a good predictor for how therapy will go. So finding the "right fit" is important. Be sure not to worry about their feelings: You are the consumer and have the right to choose the therapist you want. Don't give up on therapy itself, though, just because the first attempts were not marvelous. Some people interview three or four therapists before they pick the one with whom to work. Professionals understand this fact and are not offended if you choose to go elsewhere. Many will even give you a list of names to try.

(2) **Do I agree with his methods?** Is the therapist respectful of your Christian beliefs? Does he understand them sufficiently to be of help to you? Many non-Christian therapists will respect your faith and, though not personally

142

acquainted with it, may be able to work well with you. Some Christian therapists, while genuine believers, do not integrate their beliefs into their therapy at all; others integrate it thoroughly. You have a right to ask what they do.

(3) **Does this therapist see me as an active participant in the therapy?** Or does he come across as if I am to do just what he says with no input as to goals or type of treatment offered? We tell clients that the more that they put into therapy, the more they will get out of it, and that we expect their active participation.

(4) **What are my own goals for therapy?** What do I want to accomplish? Does this therapist seem qualified to meet my needs? Generally, there are three types of therapists: psychiatrists, psychologists, and various masters-level people. Psychiatrists are medical doctors who can prescribe medicines as well as do therapy. Some are interested in doing therapy; others prefer only to work with medications, referring the actual therapy to others. Psychologists are also doctoral level people who have been licensed by the state to practice psychology. They are not qualified to give medications. The various masters-level people are usually licensed clinical social workers (M.S.W.—Masters in Social Work), licensed marriage and family therapists (M.F.T.—Masters in Family Therapy), and other masters degree holders such as Masters in Counseling and Guidance, Masters in Counselor Education, Masters in Psychology, Masters in Psychiatric Nursing. Normally, each state has particular requirements for each category. It is usually preferable to see a licensed person, or someone supervised closely by a licensed person. Most insurance companies only reimburse for therapy by a psychiatrist or psychologist. If you believe you may need medicine or hospitalization, be sure that if you see someone other than a psychiatrist, your therapist has referral sources available to meet your needs while in treatment/therapy with him.

WHAT RECOVERY LOOKS LIKE

Discovering the "Real Thing"

How can people know if they are recovering? What behaviors, attitudes, feelings do recovering people have? How can you tell a codependent response from a generally unselfish gesture?

The following eight principles can be used as guidelines in this matter of discerning the differences between codependent "love" and genuine love:

(1) **A person cannot give what he has not received.** In Christianity we emphasize giving to others and being selfless, not being selfish. The problem is that we are usually asking people to give away something they have not received. Donald Sloat in his fine book *The Dangers of Growing Up in a Christian Home*, quotes Paul Tournier in the use of the term "premature renunciation."[11] He examines how in our well-meaning attempts to train children properly, we teach them to renounce everything for others, as if doing anything for oneself is bad, evil, and selfish. Look at the Sunday school papers, children's storybooks, or songs we teach children. Rarely do we see a child being happy doing something for himself, enjoying a new hat or toy, saying no, or acting like a normal child. The "good child" is the one who gives up his toy for his friend; who lets someone else have the last cookie; who helps others, yet is never helped or befriended himself. Sloat points out that such modeling results in the child coming to believe that "anything for me is wrong and will displease Jesus." Thus, sin becomes defined emotionally as "anything I want or need myself."

Yet, as Sloat also points out, this emphasis on premature renunciation is contrary to the way in which God created us to function. Normal childhood development requires that a child (at age two) say no and learn to appreciate things as "mine." To meaningfully be able to give later in life, two-year-olds need to establish in their minds what is theirs and

144

learn to be independent of others' needs and wants. For example, if a child learns that there are certain things that are his, and it is not selfish to enjoy them, then later when he is cognitively older, the concept of sharing makes sense. He then shares out of love, not out of obligation, and when he does, it has meaning. How meaningful is it if I give you a pen that I don't value because I don't believe I deserve to have it anyway? But if I know this is *my* pen and I *love* it, yet I choose to loan it to you or give it to you—is not that real love? We inadvertently teach children to give things away before they have learned to possess them. Sloat states and I agree wholeheartedly:

> . . . teaching children to give up things before they have learned to possess them (renunciation), or to put themselves last before they have mastered self-assertion, creates a feeling of low self-worth. . .in reality self-assertion and renunciation are two sides of the same coin. . . .Before a person can renounce something, he must assert himself to possess it. Before he can give to another he must receive.[12]

Sloat, while talking about those raised in Christian homes, has also hit the nail on the head, so to speak, for codependent people. Even people in non-Christian families have been influenced enough by this distortion of Christianity so that they have taught it to their children. I have also seen this in clients from Roman Catholic backgrounds and realize that Protestants alone do not have this problem. Scripture says, "We love [him] because he first loved us" (1 John 4:19), yet we have forgotten that principle of receiving love *before* giving it!

Codependent people usually give out of obligation, need-iness, shame, or fear. They feel guilty for even having needs of their own, much less having them met. In the long run, their well runs dry because they have never learned to receive. If a person is giving and not receiving there is a

145

problem with the kinds of "loving" in which they are engaged.

(2) Genuine love is given freely without compulsion. A person who loves in a healthy manner recognizes that they honestly have a choice. They do not see themselves as "having to" do something. They do not give out of fear of abandonment or fear of rejection. They are not loving because God will punish them if they are not. For example, Ananias and Sapphira *gave* to the church, but God knew their hearts! But we always hear that God loves a "cheerful giver." This does not mean we will always be jumping for joy when we give as a healthy person, but rather that we recognize we have the choice *not* to give.

(3) Genuine love does not do for someone else what he could or should do for himself. For example, I know someone who still goes over to her thirty-year-old son's house every Saturday evening and polishes his shoes for him for Sunday morning! Genuine love is sometimes "tough" and makes the person grow up! How many times have you seen parents, who are elderly and really cannot afford to do so, supporting one or more grown children, who for their part refuse to work or do so only half-heartedly? When confronted, the parents cry, "But we love them so much. We couldn't bear to throw them out into the street!" Genuine love does not allow others to be dependent in a way that is unnatural or unhealthy for their stage of development.

(4) Genuine love respects the other's right to refuse "help" or "love." It waits to be asked or offers aid tentatively. Genuine love never takes away another's self-respect. Here is an example of a nonrespectful, however well-meaning gesture: A mother came over to her newly married daughter's apartment with a ham, four steaks, a chuck roast, and two chickens. She said, "I brought some things for your freezer." She had not called ahead to ask if the daughter had room in the freezer, much less whether she needed the food! The daughter was quite angry and felt demeaned that her mother was trying to supplement their food supply. She felt hurt that her mother seemingly didn't believe her husband could provide for them.

(5) **Genuine love does not enable someone to stay in a destructive lifestyle or situation**. Many parents unwittingly enable their children to stay on drugs, keep on missing classes, or in some way be irresponsible. For example, a young man graduates from a two-year associates degree program in drafting. His parents continue to pay for his apartment in the college town although he refuses to look for work, has not even started a resumé, is very depressed and sits around drinking and watching TV all day.

Another example: a wife answers the phone for her husband because he is too hung over to talk. She tells the pastor that he has the flu, and will not be able to come to the elders meeting that evening. It never occurs to her to tell the pastor the truth or to let the husband handle the phone call himself. Enabling someone means allowing him to escape the consequences of his own behavior. Genuine love is tough enough to let others face their own consequences. It does not rescue or enable a person inappropriately.

(6) **Genuine love is balanced in regard to giving and receiving**. Codependent love is usually very one-sided: the codependent gives; the other receives. While even in healthy relationships one person may give more than the other at times, there is always a swing back to a balance of giving and receiving. Even when the person receiving is not able to give back in kind, there is a healthy receiving on the giver's part. The example that comes to mind is Mother Teresa. She gives selflessly to those who cannot give back to her *in kind*. Yet, she herself receives from them love, warmth, genuine affection, or perhaps merely a sigh of relief. This is not to say there is no place for giving to enemies or to those who will not give anything back. But that type of giving is costly. Only Jesus had the capability to give so perfectly *all* the time; and *even He* needed to receive sustenance from God the Father, the

147

angels, and His friends. Yet, codependent people think they should give as He gave *without* receiving sustenance or help from anyone! They believe they do not deserve aid or help or refreshment, that somehow suffering alone as martyrs is better than working with other Christians.

(7) **Genuine love is giving as much as is humanly possible for the good of another, without a self-serving payoff**. This is a touchy principle because codependent people always claim that their behaviors toward others are for the other's good. In reality, however, often these behaviors infringe on the other's rights or responsibilities, or are done out of fear not love. An example of genuine love would be parents telling their minor child that he is not allowed to associate with certain hoodlums in the neighborhood. While the parents might have some realistic fear behind this type of action, their primary motive is for the child's good because they recognize he is a child and is unable to see the dangers involved. An example of the codependent type of "love" would be the wife who pours her alcoholic husband's booze down the toilet. Managing his alcohol use is his responsibility. He is an adult, and her actions infringe on his responsibility for himself. Also, she is not so much motivated for him as for herself. She's afraid he'll get drunk and leave her or go be with another woman. While very unpleasant, these things are not *hers* to control, but his. Pouring the liquor down the toilet also lets him escape the consequences of his drunken behavior. Her motive was not out of love, but fear, and out of a need to control him rather than let him learn to control himself.

(8) **Genuine love comes from the Holy Spirit, not from self-effort**. Self-effort produces a "love" characterized by self-righteousness, and a "martyr-spirit." For example, "Look at all *I've* done for him. I've slaved for him. Worked for him. Now he's done this? How could he do this to *me*? After all I have done for him!" Love from the Holy Spirit is not concerned with receiving gratitude or thanks or appreciation.

It is genuine, selfless, and produces a sense of joy, not a sense of martyrdom.

Codependent love expects a return, if only subtly. One woman recently into recovery told me that now she can see that her efforts at being loving, her striving to be caring, her compulsion to serve or help others, especially men, all had at their foundation a fear of asking for what she needed. Her unconscious belief was *If I try hard enough, if I love enough, if I give enough, then they will know my needs without me saying anything and they will take care of me.* She added that all she ever wanted was to feel "safe" and assumed that if her parents or husband were unkind, or neglectful, it must have been because she was "bad" or had not "loved enough." This kind of "love" is produced by self-effort, not by the Holy Spirit. Obviously, its result is not joy, but pain and resentment.

SUMMARY OF THE PRINCIPLES

We have seen so far that there are eight principles which will guide us to discern the difference between codependent "love" and genuine, Christian love. In summary, they are:

(1) A person cannot give what he has not received.

(2) Genuine love is given freely without compulsion.

(3) Genuine love does not do for someone else what he could or should be doing for himself.

(4) Genuine love respects the other's right to refuse the "help" or "love."

(5) Genuine love does not "enable" another person to remain in a destructive lifestyle or situation.

(6) Genuine love is balanced in regard to giving and receiving.

(7) Genuine love is given, as much as possible, for the good of the other, without a self-serving payoff for the giver.

(8) Genuine love comes from the Holy Spirit, not self-effort.

SELF-CENTEREDNESS VS. CARING FOR ONESELF

Some people reading the literature available today on codependency are concerned that "taking care of yourself" can lead to hedonism and selfishness. Obviously, as Christians, we are concerned about having a balance between legitimate self-care and care for others. All of us, if we are honest, are sinful enough, in our worst moments, to want to control and manipulate others. We want our own way, want to control others, if only out of fear. This type of response, albeit understandable, is not loving. All of us have seen in ourselves or in others the swing to the anti-dependent lifestyle, as shown in figure 8. This position is usually taken by someone who is either burned out on being dependent (left side of the scale) or who is terrified of being dependent. This approach is what we usually think of as selfish: The person who *only* thinks of himself; who *forces* others to do things his way; who acts like he does not need anyone.

Yet, is not the codependent person who is acting needy; who manipulates through kindness and guilt; who controls others with smiles and by making others dependent on him— is not this person equally selfish? Is it really acting out of genuine love to do things for someone solely out of fear of abandonment or rejection? Is it less selfish to control others by doing things for them that they should do for themselves? In my work with hundreds of codependent people, I have never seen one who was in danger of becoming hedonistic. For them, the danger is in remaining blind to the inherent selfishness of trying to put someone else or something else at the center of their life, other than God Himself. Others are not loved in a codependent relationship because of who they are, but for how they make the codependent feel. Codependent people love to feel needed and often only feel worth-

150

Figure 10: Two Styles of Selfishness

The Root Causes of
Shame and Fear of Abandonment
Produce:
A need to control others
A need to manipulate others
A need to have one's own way

This Results in Two Styles of Selfish Behavior

Codependent "Love"	Domineering "Love"
Person feels obsessed but acts more quiet in a subtle, undercover, manner; does things for others "for their own good", manipulates through niceness, kindness, doing "nice," "loving" things to "earn" love from others or to control them. Pouts, uses "guilt trips" to control, feels unworthy, needy, starved for love and attention, plays victim, acts helpless when all else fails to get what they want. Wants others to be just as obsessed with them as they are with others; feels reluctant or guilty about receiving.	Acts cold, unfeeling; doesn't "need" anything; forces others through meanness, brute force, yelling, or power plays to do things their way. Unaware of own inner pain, or own need for love and attention. Despises people who look needy; is terrified of being dependent or needy. Even legitimate needs are perceived as weaknesses. Wants admiration and obedience. Believe they do things because they know what is best for others. Demand that others give to them.

while if someone needs them or if they have something to worry about or upon which to focus. Codependent people who go into recovery are always stunned at how controlling and manipulative (selfish) they have been. They also want someone else to be as obsessed with them as they are with the other person. Obsession *is* love to them, and so if they "love" someone, they are obsessed with them, and feel "hurt" or "rejected" if the obsessive attention is not returned.

Thus, while codependent people look more "loving" outwardly, their heart reveals just as much root-selfishness as the more domineering individuals (see figure 10).

BALANCE VERSUS IMBALANCE

The issue of learning to care for oneself, as well as others, is not one of selfishness versus unselfishness, but rather of balance vs. imbalance. Both the domineering "love" style and the codependent "love" style are imbalanced or distorted. Genuine love gives and receives. Christ calls us to love our neighbor "as our self." All of us have innate tendencies to be selfish and controlling no matter which style we choose. Learning to care for oneself and for others involves becoming interdependent (see figure 8). The analogy of the body of Christ is appropriate here. Paul, in 1 Corinthians 12, skillfully sketches an image of our spiritual union with others being like the physical unity of the human body. Each part is valuable, necessary, and dependent on the other parts. He encourages us to see the beauty hidden in even the less outwardly beautiful parts of the body. Codependent people at times, however, are a lot like the eye or ear that would cry out, "If I am not the feet, I am not valuable to the body." Or at other times, they are like a rebellious foot walking alone without the aid of the other foot, without the support of the legs or ankles! Codependent people usually grew up in families where they could not depend on others physically and/or emotionally. They were left on their own in some way, so naturally, they never learned to be interdependent because no one ever modeled giving and receiving. For many of them, the only adults they knew were "takers," who, for whatever reason, could not or would not give to their child. We can only learn to receive if someone models it for us. Often codependent people find that a therapist is the first person who has ever given to them freely, without a self-serving payoff. A number of people have commented ruefully to me, "It's too bad—sad really—that I had to *pay* someone to love me unconditionally." Unfortunately, the Christian community is not always open, nonjudgmental, or accepting enough for these folks to have found this type of acceptance in the church. Scores of codependent people have shared with me heartbreaking stories of rejection, ridicule, and judgment from churches and so-called Christians from whom they had sought unconditional love. Jesus calls us to love one another so the world will know we are His disciples. Sometimes I wonder what the world thinks when it hears stories like the ones I hear every day!

UNDERSTANDING GENUINE GIVING

Richard Foster in his book *Celebration of Discipline: The Path to Spiritual Growth* does a masterful job at distinguishing "self-righteous service" (which I will call "codependent giving") from what he calls "true giving"[13] (which I will call "genuine service"). In the following chart, I have defined both kinds of service to focus their differences. Codependent giving comes from self-effort and is based on the codependent "love" mentioned previously. Genuine giving comes from the work of God in us through the Holy Spirit and is not based on selfishness.

As we have seen, there is quite a difference between codependent "love" and genuine love, as well as codependent giving and genuine giving. None of us, codependent or not, can love with genuine love without the power of God.

153

FIGURE 11

Understanding Genuine Service

Codependent Service

Service comes from self-effort and involves a sense of frantic striving and fervor.

Person enjoys serving, especially if the task is monumental and is a "big deal." May seem falsely modest or humble.

Person requires external results, rewards, appreciation, human response. Needs attention, recognition, and wants others to reciprocate.

Person picks when, where, whom to serve, depending on what the resulting feedback will be or on what they, as givers, need to feel or receive. Feelings dominate the serving.

Service becomes a role, an identity, a way of feeling "good" about oneself, and a way to maintain the martyr position in life.

Person does not let the other take responsibility for himself; tries to control the other; does things for the other without asking if he thinks the other person wants or needs the help.

Person gives service or "love" only to others, not to self; Thus, the giver eventually feels burned out, used up, resentful, bitter.

Service makes the giver feel safe and powerful, makes the receiver feel weak, insecure, victimized and dependent. Fractures community through manipulation.

Genuine Service

Service comes from inner prompting of the Holy Spirit and while energy is expended there is no frantic or frenzied compulsion.

Person enjoys all service regardless of how small or seemingly unimportant. Is genuinely modest and acts out of joy of service.

Person is content to remain unnoticed, hidden, unappreciated; does not need recognition. Does not mind attention, but doesn't need it.

Person is indiscriminate, i.e., serves anyone at any time, regardless of the other's position, ability to reciprocate, or of his own need to be admired, or his own momentary feelings.

Service has its roots in an identity firmly grounded in God's love and image within the person.

Person takes responsibility for self, lets others be responsible for themselves. Lets go of the other; appreciates all things and people for what they are in relation to the self.

Person is interdependent and balanced in giving and receiving, knows when it is appropriate to temporarily squelch one's own needs and desires to assume total responsibility for someone else (e.g. for infants or severely ill people), and when to let others give to them.

The giver and receiver have a reciprocal relationship. Serves without putting others under obligation. Builds unity in relationships. Heals, doesn't tear down community.

That is why letting go of control and giving our will and life to God is so very crucial. People who have lived a codependent lifestyle as a way to feel whole, strong, or secure will find that relinquishing it is a day-to-day, spiritual, and emotional battle. Thus, recovery is a continual lifelong process, which will require discipline and courage. It cannot, as we have seen, be done alone. We need to have the support of those around us, especially those in the church. Chapter 8 will examine the role of the Christian community in the development of and recovery from codependency.

DEVELOPING HEALTHY RELATIONSHIPS

Once persons are in recovery, they inevitably ask me, "Well, what does a healthy relationship look like anyway?" It's not such a surprising question because they may never have experienced a healthy interpersonal relationship. They may have lacked the necessary modeling in their family of origin to be able to understand how to identify and be comfortable in such a relationship. They do know that codependent behavior has been a destructive style of life and that now that they are recovering it's important for them to make different choices and live differently, but they are still confused as to what a healthy relationship is. Some people are even skeptical that a healthy relationship for themselves is possible. One of my former supervisors, Dr. Will Caradine, said that everyone has some neurotic content in his marriage, but there is a difference between relationships that survive and those that fail. In the relationships that survive, the involved persons are willing to face their neurosis and deal with their problems; in relationships that fail, partners refuse to admit problems, face their shortcomings, and deal with them. So, given the fact that no one—not even therapists—can have perfectly flawless relationships, what can we aim for if we want to be healthy in our relationships to others, especially in marriage?

155

There are so many books about marriage in the bookstores these days that it's hard to keep up with them all. Many, many people have researched the myriad aspects of the marital relationship. One recent bit of research in particular has. interested me. After studying many successful long-term relationships, Francine Klagsburn, in *Married People: Staying Together in An Age of Divorce*, presents eight common characteristics of successful marriages.

---

(1) An ability to change and tolerate change
(2) A willingness to live with what you cannot change
(3) An assumption of permanence about the relationship
(4) Trust between the partners
(5) A balance of depending on each other (interdependence)
(6) A balance of power in the relationship
(7) An enjoyment of each other (friendship)
(8) A shared history that is cherished[14]

When I read this list, I was struck by the similarity between Klagsburn's characteristics and the steps that my successful clients have taken when they rebuild their relationships with friends, family members, and marriage partners. Notice how these steps coincide with Klagsburn's characteristics:

STEPS TO A HEALTHY RELATIONSHIP

(1) Recognize that you can only change yourself, not the other person. Years ago, Evelyn Christiansen wrote a small book on prayer entitled, *Lord, Change Me!* She was right! So often in our prayers, we ask God to change the other person, but we are reluctant to have Him work on us. Accepting others as they are and letting go of our need to control them is crucial! The following anonymous poem has been making the rounds of various newsletters, pamphlets, and recovery literature lately. I think it aptly describes what "letting go" is like in real life!

TO "LET GO" TAKES LOVE

To "let go" does not mean to stop caring, it means that I can't do it for someone else.

To "let go" is not to cut myself off, it is the realization that I can't control another.

To "let go" is not to enable, but to allow learning from natural consequences.

To "let go" is to admit powerlessness, which means the outcome is not in my hands.

To "let go" is not to try to change or blame another, it is to make the most of myself.

To "let go" is not to care for, but to care about.

To "let go" is not to fix, but to be supportive.

To "let go" is not to judge, but to allow another to be a human being.

To "let go" is not to be in the middle arranging all the outcomes but to allow others to effect their own destinies.

To "let go" is not to be protective, it is to permit another to face reality.

To "let go" is not to deny, but to accept.

To "let go" is not to nag, scold, or argue, but instead to search out my own shortcomings and to correct them.

To "let go" is not to adjust everything to my desires but to take each day as it comes, and to cherish myself in it.

To "let go" is not to criticize and regulate anybody but to try to become what I dream I can be.

To "let go" is not to regret the past, but to grow and to live for the future.

To "let go" is to fear less and to love more.

(2) **Make a genuine commitment to the relationship.** This second step toward a healthy relationship seems difficult for many people today. Steven Carter has even written a book

157

Men Who Can't Love which tells how to spot a man who is unable to commit to a permanent relationship![15] Even for Christians there seems to be a reluctance to make a deep commitment. The attitude seems to be "when the going gets tough. . .I'll get going. . .to the divorce court!" While I do understand that in this age of adultery and desertion there are times when, even for Christians, divorce becomes the lesser of two evils, it seems to me that people today are too quick to bail out when things get difficult. The fact is that life is not fair. We don't always get what we want or feel we deserve. Successful married life takes two commitments before God: commitment to your spouse and commitment to marriage as an institution. Each of these commitments are necessary to ensure that marriage can work. When things get rough in the relationship, then you must rely on your commitment to the institution of marriage itself. When marriage itself seems boring, confining, or stupid, then your commitment to the other person pulls you through. Every marriage has struggles. Every spouse wishes at times that they had never met the other person, just as every parent wishes at times that they could trade in their kids for a new sports car or a mink coat! Why do we assume we can be unconditionally supportive of our children and remain committed to them even if they hurt us but say we "can't" do that for the child's parent—our spouse? Again, I realize that circumstances do come up where because of physical, sexual, or emotional abuse, repeated adulteries, or desertion that such a commitment is no longer possible. It takes two to make that type of commitment. Yet, how can a relationship grow if you are never sure that the other person will be there for you even when you fail? Relationships can recover from abuse, from adultery, from neglect. It takes courage, work, and the commitment of *both* people but it can happen.

(3) **Decide to trust the other person.** Trust is a decision first, then a feeling. If I wait to trust someone until I feel trusting, I will probably never do it. Trust is a gift you give

unless it is proven over time that the other is unreliable. Trust is probably the most difficult thing to rebuild in a marriage (or in any relationship) once it has been broken. The biggest stumbling block though seems to be the need we have to *feel* trusting. I can trust someone, however, even when I feel doubtful. The doubtful feelings come from a habit which developed over time. It will take a while for those feelings to disappear, just as it takes time to adjust to driving in England. For a time while driving on the left side of the road, you say to yourself, *I'm doing the right thing but it feels wrong.* And you concentrate, ignoring the discomfort, maintaining your driving on the left. Eventually the feelings catch up, and you feel just fine driving on the left. So it is with trust. You decide to trust, and to do so—despite feelings of doubt—until the evidence stacks up in one of two directions, either for the decision to trust, or against it. Sometimes our intuition is right about distrusting someone, sometimes it is not. Thus, we wait for the evidence.

(4) **Learn to be interdependent and allow for a balance of power in the relationship**. No relationship will be healthy when one person is always dominant and the other subservient. No one can be in "the one-down" position for very long without a great deal of pain and resentment building up, if only unconsciously. Healthy people know both how to give and to receive. Neither one in the relationship is on a power trip, trying to control giving or receiving. (My tape series *Male-Female Relationships: Discovering Unhealthy Patterns*[16] covers this point in great detail if you want further information.)

(5) **Develop a friendship over time**. Our society likes things instantly: instant mashed potatoes, instant money machines, instant coffee. Healthy relationships are like brewed coffee: They take time, fill a home with a fragrant aroma, and if brewed carefully, never leave a bitter taste in your mouth! Some people have never had a relationship that lasted more than a few years, other than with a parent or

FIGURE 12
CODEPENDENCY RECOVERY

THERAPY

SUPPORT
GROUPS

SPIRITUAL
DEVELOPMENT

12 -STEP WORK

SUPPORTIVE
WORK
ENVIRONMENT

FAMILY LIFE

sibling. Our society is so mobile that many children have not had the chance to develop long-term friendships. Rarely do they get to see grandparents or aunts and uncles celebrating thirty-five or fifty years of marriage. Yet real friendship involves having a cherished, shared history, and history takes time. When I hear of people who divorce after only two or three years of marriage, I feel sad because I realize they barely got to know each other!

Friendship occurs, not only when we have time together with someone, but also when we do *pleasant things with* them! If all you do with your spouse is clean the house or change diapers, then you are in trouble! We tend to associate pleasant feelings with the people with whom we experience something enjoyable. If I like golf and I always golf with my friend Susie, than I will tend to associate her with my pleasant feelings about golf. The problem a lot of marriages have is that all the pleasant experiences are associated with the wrong people! Willard Harley in his book *His Needs, Her Needs: Building an Affair-Proof Marriage* encourages couples to become each other's "recreational companions."[17] I could not agree more! As he points out, there is so little time we can spend relaxing, why should we do it in a way that *excludes* our spouse!

SUMMARY

We have seen that recovery involves a number of overlapping areas: Twelve-Step work, support groups, therapy, spiritual development, family life, and other relationships, such as friends at work or school. In chapter 8 we will examine more closely the role of the Christian community in addiction and recovery.

8

CODEPENDENCY AND THE CHURCH COMMUNITY

So far, we have focused primarily on codependency as a phenomenon involving individuals and small groups such as the family. In reality, however, codependent behaviors can be seen in organizations as well. In fact, organizations can be addictive, too.

We have all seen people who seem addicted to their work. For them, "the company" has become the central focus of their life. They are totally preoccupied with it. They focus on it so much as to lose contact with other important aspects of their lives. They actually feel as if they would die if they had to stop work or retire. Without their company, life feels meaningless to them.

Church, too, can be the focus of someone's life so much so that it becomes an actual addiction. While this may appear shocking to some, this phenomenon is all too common to those in the Christian counseling arena.

A Case Study

Take the mother of one of my clients, we'll call her Martha. Martha is between fifty-five and sixty years old and has three grown children. Her first husband, the father of her children, was an alcoholic. She divorced him when the youngest child was two years old. Some years later her ex-husband committed suicide, as did her own father. When her youngest child was six or seven, she remarried and her new husband adopted the kids. During their high-school years, the children became Christians. Some years later after all three children were grown, Martha accepted Christ also. Her spouse at first was open to her newfound faith but later became antagonistic because of Martha's "pushy" behavior. Her children began to notice changes in her lifestyle and were concerned that she was becoming addicted to religiosity.

Prior to becoming a Christian, Martha had done lots of social and recreational things with her husband. She would golf, bowl, and fish. She had a lively circle of friends with whom she shared these activities. One to entertain, Martha would host their friends in the family home, as well as go with her spouse to their homes. She was an avid house cleaner. Everything was neat and tidy. On holidays she enjoyed her family and encouraged them to come home. She would cook nice meals, especially for Easter or Christmas Eve.

Since her conversion, however, Martha has changed. One by one she has dropped old friends. Presently, she has no friends outside the church. Golfing, bowling, and fishing have been replaced by compulsive piano practicing, "so I can be prepared for Sunday" when she plays for the church service. She no longer does anything with her husband, but spends all her evenings (and some days) at the church. Her home that used to be fastidiously kept is now a "disaster area" according to her son. Yet, Martha finds time to take one day a week to clean at the church. On Sundays she is gone almost all day despite the fact that her husband sits home alone. She goes to Sunday school, church, coffee social, and then comes home for two hours. She rests and then goes back for the rest of the afternoon and evening. She has become compulsive about

163

church attendance: Once when her son and daughter-in-law from out-of-town were visiting for a day or so, they chose to go fishing with her husband rather than attend church, since their time with him was so short. When she came home in the evening from church (not having spent any time with her son and his wife) and learned that they had not caught any fish that morning, she self-righteously proclaimed, "See I *knew* you would not catch any because you did not go to church." Another time, when she was going out the door to another church function, her daughter-in-law said, "Have fun!" To which Martha replied, "I am *not* having fun! I am going to serve the Lord!"

Her relationships within the family have soured. At church she is sweet, kindly, loving, and giving. She will go to any ends to meet the needs of other parishioners. Yet on Christmas Eve she refused to cook (she was gone all day and evening at church) or to tell others what they could do to help prepare a nice meal, or even to let them know when she'd be home. Finally, they gave up waiting for her and ordered pizza!

Her children report that her pastor and church friends would be shocked to see the difference between her behavior at home and at church. At home, she is full of anger, force-feeds Christianity to her husband, acts bossy and irritable, demanding her way and engaging in heated battles to get it. At church, her nonverbals are gentle, less authoritarian. She acts sweet and loving, kind to everyone.

Martha's children and husband are concerned about how her church activities consume her life. She neglects her husband, children, and grandchildren because of these activities. One time recently, my client and spouse went up to visit Martha and her husband. They had sacrificed considerably in terms of time and finances to make this trip. The entire two to three days they were there, Martha kept coming and going to church, refused to sit down and talk to them, did not cook meals, and refused to play games or cards. She claimed that she "had to" be at every church function; that it was her duty as a good Christian. Around the house, even when she is not home, Martha plays Christian music on the radio. Every radio is tuned to a Christian station, and although her husband loudly protests, she insists on leaving it on. It is as if she needs to fill her mind constantly with religious jargon and input.

Martha exhibits all the characteristics of an addicted person. She is consumed by her religious activity. She has lost interest in good friends and activities that she used to enjoy. She acts one way when she is having her "fix" (being in church) and another when deprived of it (while at home). It has cost Martha her joy, so it obviously is done not for pleasure, but to escape pain. Stuck in denial, she is unable to see the clearly destructive pattern of her behavior. When confronted by her oldest child regarding the unbiblical nature of some of her behavior and attitudes, she reacted angrily, told him to "shut up," and stormed out of the house. When another child tried to lovingly point out the same things at a different time, she switched roles and instead of getting angry, played victim. She whined, "But you don't understand how hard it is to live with your father. He treats me so terribly." Instead of facing the pain in her marriage, Martha is using church as a distraction, as a sedative, as an addiction.

PROMISES AND CONTROL

Martha is just one example of a person who is using the church as an addictive substance. Schaef and Fassel[1] in their research on addictive organizations have discovered some ways that organizations function as addictive "substances." Two key ways are the "promises" made to members, and control. Let's see how these two methods work in a church, which is, of course, an organization.

In an addictive system, the "promise" is that something about being involved with the system—whether it be a drugs system, a family system, or an organizational system—will enable you to escape the "here and now" experiences of life. It focuses you on what "could be" or what "may be" if only this or that will happen. "If you use this chemical, you'll feel better, perform better, socialize better." "If you join our team, you'll be accepted, popular. You'll belong—you'll be one of us." "If you do things our way, you'll gain recognition, approval, a chance to develop social skills, caring, success." The promise is that you won't have to deal with what *is*, with the real life pain or sadness you are experiencing. The promise, while not always overt, is there underneath everything else, beckoning to people. "Join our team! Then you'll find success, happiness, peace, security, a sense of worth."[2]

Is this not how Christianity is portrayed all too often? Rather than a call to discipleship, the call is to "easy salvation," to a "fix-it" mentality type of faith. "Come to Jesus. Find in Him peace and happiness." "Join our church. We follow the *true* biblical path. With us, you will find a new family, a new home, a new identity. Stick with us and we'll give you purpose and meaning. You can help win the world for Christ by the year 2000!"

A proviso: in no way do I mean to denigrate the fact that in Christ, as a result of a true encounter with God Incarnate, we can find peace, security, and a sense of meaning to life. The Scripture points clearly to the fact that without Him, we can do nothing! We also see in Scripture a picture of the body of Christ as a family—God's own household. We know that if Father and Mother "forsake" us, the Lord will "take us up" (Ps. 27:10). Yet, what I want to point out is the power of a promise. Even when the promise is itself genuine, it can be presented in a distorted manner, and it can be heard in a distorted manner.

For example, it may be that the church members who "fit in" the best in our evangelical churches are those who come from dysfunctional families! These people have let the promise beguile them into creating new families. For example, they hope to receive in the church fellowship what they never received in childhood: security, recognition, caring, praise, modeling, and more. Thus, they do everything they have to in order to fit in—just as they did in childhood. They comply; they play by the rules; they discover what the right thing to do or *not* do is, and then do it or *don't* do it. They are constantly tuned in to what is expected and dare not veer off the path for fear of losing this family, too. It may well be that those who are uncomfortable with the "party line," with being so rigidly a "team-player," end up feeling uneasy in the church, do not advance into leadership circles, and after a while, leave. Maybe this is why our churches tend to be so homogenous!

The other main mechanism used by organizations to function addictively is control. We can all identify with this one! Without hardly thinking about it, I bet you could tell me what the "rules" are about dress code in your church. No one may have ever said so, but you know slacks are forbidden Sunday morning but okay at prayer meeting or Sunday evening. In most churches a man without a tie and jacket sticks out like a sore thumb. Everyone knows that acceptance into the "church family" is earned by doing things the "right way," for example, the way your particular church or denomination has decided is the "right way!" A dear friend of ours is a new Christian. He recently went to a Christian discipleship seminar. He was startled to meet Christians who did not drink once in a while, or could not say "damn" when frustrated or angry! He startled the entire group when he remarked that he liked the writings of Paul better than the Gospels because Jesus seemed to be "laid back" whereas "Paul knew how to kick a !!" Everyone just roared with laughter! It's kind of sad in a way, that in a year or so, our friend, if he wants to fit in, will have become somewhat less real, less colorful, and more boring—more like us!

There is a sense where membership (i.e., a sense of belonging/acceptance, not "formal membership") in the

167

church often depends on being less yourself and more like everyone else. If you are yourself, and do not follow the party line, you may risk being ostracized.

Years ago, I belonged to a large evangelical church and was a part of their large, mostly volunteer "student staff." My dear friend and then pastor tried to encourage me to seek other opportunities because the approach in that particular ministry was so rigid. At the time, I resisted this notion, claiming I needed the structure. Some months later, I did, however, move to another city to be on the staff of another church. Some of the people from my former church came to present a discipleship seminar. After the seminar I asked one of the staff at my present church what he thought of them. I can still remember his comment, "Well, what they had to say was fine, but they all seemed to be clones of the leaders—right down to the beige corduroy jackets, briefcases, and ties for the men, and skirts, blouses, neck scarves, and canvas book bags for the women!" I laughed too and began to see that my pastor was right: There really *was* too much rigidity in that organization.

A LOFTY MISSION

Schaef and Fassel[3] in their research on organizations as addictive "substances," also have noted that there is an inverse correlation between the loftiness of the organization's mission and the congruence between its stated and unstated goals. They have noticed that usually when this lack of congruence occurs, the organization will enter into a rigid denial system, which becomes grandiose in itself. (Grandiosity means pretending to be more than or something other than what you actually are.)

In their book, *The Addictive Organization*, Schaef and Fassel report that "helping" organizations (such as churches, schools, hospitals) often refuse to make their mission statement realistic. They want it to be vague and abstract because they do not want to face the pain of noticing how few of their members ever achieve it, or that in reality they see little or few changes, or change is so slow as to be barely noticeable. If the mission statement remains lofty, grandiose, and exalted, it acts like a "fix." It reassures the members of the organization that they are important and have value because they do important work.[4]

Isn't that just what we see in our church and even parachurch organizations? Most church bodies are so vague about their mission statement as not to have one! Ask the average evangelical church-goer what the purpose of his church is, and you'll get as many answers as there are church-goers! Denial is rampant in our churches—and among Christians too. For example, during this year alone I have encountered in my practice seven people, all of whom although "born again," "baptized in the Holy Spirit," and/or "filled with the Spirit"—have problems with chronic lying! For three or four, the problem is bad enough to be considered a major personality disorder! Yet, all these people espouse love for the Lord, have held or do hold positions in the church, and would be quite offended if someone questioned the veracity of their faith. These people are being grandiose in exactly the sense Schaef and Fassel speak of in their book.[5] And the churches these people belong to call on them to continue on pretending to be "more than or other than" what they actually are! No one wants to rock the boat and notice that not only are they not moving, but in reality, the boat may be on the verge of sinking. For these people, Christianity has become an addictive experience—a way to mediate their shame without really changing their behavior.

ADDICTIVE RELIGION VERSUS
HEALTHY RELIGION

As William Lenters says in his book *The Freedom We Crave: Addiction—The Human Condition*, religious experience can become addictive because we, as human beings,

FIGURE 13

ADDICTIVE RELIGIOSITY VS. HEALTHY FAITH

Codependency-Prone Religiosity

1. Participants have an ill-defined sense of self. They expect the religious experience to tell them who they are, what they need, what they want, what they feel. They lack self assurance.

2. Causes one to become dependent, to escape personal responsibilites, to escape personal choice. Everything is predetermined by the church, group, or fellowship.

3. Participants want everything black or white, right or wrong. A compartmentalizing of life occurs. Some religious behaviors are regarded as spiritual and all important but are not necessarily connected to everyday life. Thus a person could follow all the rules publically, but act-out privately and deny the discrepency.

4. Participants look to the religious experience to deliver them from their powerlessness. There is a tendency to live vicariously through a great spiritual leader, or through a distinct doctrine or ritual (Baptism, filling of Holy Spirit, etc.).

5. Believers and the "religious system" tend to be arrogant and unteachable. They see themselves as "right" and are threatened by alternative viewpoints.

6. Promotes magical thinking: "If I just pray, everything will be okay." Life is a cosmic guessing game. The object is to "psych out" and do "God's will". If I do the "right things" then my life will go well, otherwise I'm disillusioned.

7. Tends to minimize the role of the individual and individual effort, e.g.,"The Devil made me do it" or "I surrendered all to Jesus. It's not me anymore. He does everything."

Mature, Healthy Faith Experience

1. The participant has a well-defined sense of self; knows who he is, what he wants, needs, thinks, or feels. Does not look to others for self-definition.

2. Enables a person to take personal responsibility for choices; to look to God personally - without over-reliance on authority figures.

3. Allows for paradoxes in the life of faith; recognizes that not everything is black or white; that some things are unknown or ambiguous. Allows for a certain amount of reflective doubt; an openness to discussion; calls for integrated living.

4. Believers regard God not as a cosmic rescuer, but as Lord, Creator, Sovereign. He is adored and obeyed because He is GOD, not because He gives peace, or relief from problems. Leaders are seen as fellow, fallible, human beings.

5. Participants and the "religious system" are open, teachable. They recognize that there are a number of ways Scripture can legitimately be interpreted.

6. Obedience comes not from magical thinking or as a ploy to gain God's approval, but from an actual grace experience and an understanding of His mercy, based on Scripture.

7. Achieves a balance between what God does and what we are responsible to do. "Work out your salvation with fear and trembling, for it is God who works in you both to will and to work

©1989 Margaret J. Rinck

tend to lose sight of "dynamic religious experience" and develop a harmful dependence on religious belief and practices. Instead of our religious life freeing us to love as Christ loved because of God's active participation in our own lives, we become caught up in a dependency on rules, behaviors, beliefs, and dogmas.[6]

How can we differentiate neurotic, dependency-prone religion and healthy faith? What characterizes a mature, healthy faith experience versus a codependency relationship to faith? Lenters[7] sets out some helpful criteria in his work. I have expanded on his list to create the list of characteristics in figure 13.

CHRISTIAN LEADERS AS ADDICTS

Studies of organizational behavior tell us that organizations tend to take on the characteristics of their key executives. Some studies even indicate that any *key* person in the organization can set the tone for the system. This is especially true when the key person(s) are addicted themselves. Whether their addiction is chemical, relational, work-related, or "helping" others, these key addicted people have tremendous influence. It is the nature of an addiction to draw attention to the one addicted. Tremendous energy of both people and the organizational system is used focusing on the addict and the "wake" they leave behind them. Also, as Schaef and Fassel point out, addicted people tend to act in a manner that is difficult for others to understand, and begin to cut themselves off from the normal feedback mechanisms of the organization. Thus communication is both confused and quite limited. They note that the higher an addicted person is in the organization, the less their behavior is scrutinized and the more this isolation and lack of feedback grows.

Obviously, the church is an organization and operates much as other organizations do. When key people in a church have some sort of addiction, it can drastically affect everyone in the system. In a sense, the whole church as a system and individuals within the system start acting codependently just like members of a dysfunctional family do when a member becomes addicted.

Unfortunately, the restrictive rules that operate in a dysfunctional family also operate in the "church family": "don't talk," "don't feel," "don't trust." Thus, parishioners are afraid to trust their gut-level feelings or intuitions about the addict's behavior. They doubt themselves rather than question the other person. They may talk to one another, but never talk to the addict. They become afraid to trust others because of fear of being "misunderstood" or of appearing "critical" or "less spiritual" than the other people. Some suspect something is wrong, but never check out their suspicions. Others *know* what is going on but do not want to "cause trouble" for someone in leadership.

How do organizations typically handle an addicted person? Schaef and Fassel point to two main methods: more supervision (control) and/or defining the problem psychologically, thus asking the person to get help. Rarely do they see it as an addictive process. By trying to control the person more, they end up kidding themselves about the problems and have a false feeling of control. By defining it psychologically, they misdiagnose the problem, and thus misprescribe a solution.[8]

In the church, it has been my experience that there is an additional mechanism that is used to "handle" the addicted person. This additional method is to define it as a spiritual problem. Defining it psychologically may also be included with the spiritual definition. For example, a denominational church in our area had a young pastor (about twenty-eight years old). He was well-educated and enthusiastic and single. His parishioners thought he was a bit abrasive and sometimes insensitive, but they wrote it off to youth and inexperience at first. After a while, people began to notice more serious aberrant behavior and a tendency to drink too much. Again, trying to be charitable, they decided that they were being judgmental. Over a period of two years, it became clear to a number of well-informed people in the church that the pastor was indeed an alcoholic. These people went to the elder board of the church and confidentially shared their concerns. The elders had noticed the problems with his behavior but did not want to touch the alcohol issue. So they called in the denominational area director, who listened to the concerns, urged them to pray for the pastor, and approached the pastor regarding being less abrasive and more compassionate. (They were trying to define it as a spiritual problem—that if he developed more of a "pastor's heart" things would go better.) Some months passed, but "things" did not get better. So next, the denominational area personnel committee recommended that the pastor take a week's training on "Career Management" in another city. They knew this course would include psychological counseling and hoped somehow the "problem" would be solved. The pastor went, found the course interesting, and kept on drinking. (They tried to define the problem psychologically.) Months passed and the elder board decided to list certain behaviors that had to change and gave the pastor three months to "shape up." (They tried to increase the control over his behavior.) Of course, he did not change and at the end of the three months, he resigned voluntarily and was sent with their "blessings" to another church in the denomination! Alcoholism was *never* mentioned to him as the root problem. The elder board was too afraid of being sued by him for libel. So they never brought it up. Tragically, some other unsuspecting church got the "blessing" of this pastor and his alcoholism.

Schaef and Fassel point out that there are usually four ways used by people in an addictive system to relate to the addict and to each other.[9] These are similar to roles we see in alcoholic or other dysfunctional families. All these modalities are codependent in some manner. They are (1) taking a familial role, (2) exhibiting absolute denial, (3) scurrying around talking to each other but never confronting the addict, and (4) acting out. Let's apply them to the above example of the alcoholic pastor.

(1) Taking a familial role: For some in the parish, the addict was seen as the "spiritual father-figure" and hence not to be questioned. Even those who saw the problem often related to him much as children to a grumpy parent. They were afraid of him and of his "power" as pastor.

(2) Exhibiting absolute denial: These people idolized him and idealized him. There was nothing wrong with him or the church. They saw the complaints of other parishioners as ridiculous.

(3) Scurrying around talking to each other but never confronting the addict: This modality was true about all the people in the system: church members and denominational leaders. The fear of his reaction to being confronted kept them from even privately voicing a concern about the real problem.

(4) Acting out: Some people became "heroes" and tried harder to make "things" work at church, trying to make up for the pastor's failings. Others felt isolated and cut-off from the life of the church, much like "lost children" in a dysfunctional family. Some even left the church and went elsewhere. Others became the mascots or clowns and tried to cheer everyone up to get others to be less serious-minded. They were trying to help everyone feel better in the midst of a depressing situation. Like good codependents, they could not stand it to have anyone "feel bad."

We can easily see how the pastor's role as leader and spiritual guide isolated him from the feedback a person might normally be given. There is a tendency to see pastors as not quite human, so it was easy for people to deny the real nature of the problem. There had also been some question as to the sexual propriety of his behavior on a number of occasions, but *no one* wanted to touch *that one* at all!

In the meantime, a pastor in this situation is suffering. Everyone around him feeds his denial, yet inevitably the pain creeps in. It is immensely painful to live a secret life, and the amount of guilt a person in this situation feels is enormous. Getting rid of the pastor is a poor solution; however, unfortunately it is one I have seen used more than once. When this type of process is used, the congregation and its codependency is left untreated, and the system itself remains unchanged.

While some churches may identify readily with the example of an alcoholic pastor, others may not. However, the addictive pattern does not have to involve alcohol. Food and sex are two common hidden addictions in the church, not only among clergy but among parishioners. In my study of sexual addiction, experts in the field have communicated to me their concern that religious persons, and particularly clergy, can be especially vulnerable to sexual addiction. It seems that sexual addicts often use religion as a way to compensate for the great shame that they feel inside.[10] Since shame feeds addictions, the prohibition ("don't touch" and "don't talk") about sexuality in the traditional church provides a type of double bind for the sexual addict. On the one hand, sex is "forbidden," "bad" or at least not talked about much. On the other hand, there is what I call a "reverse obsession" with it. By focusing so much attention on what not to do, feel, or talk about concerning sex and sexual feelings, the church inadvertently keeps the emphasis on sex. If I tell you, "Don't think of the red monkey," what will you think about? Right! Red monkeys.

Why are clergy particularly vulnerable to sexual addiction?[11] Patrick J. Carnes, Ph.D., the leading expert in the field of sexual addiction today, has found that there are a number of occupational hazards which make clergy potentially more vulnerable to this condition. Some of these factors are:

(1) **Idealization of the pastor and other Christian leaders as more than human.** Laypeople so imbue leaders with supra-human qualities that they discount the ordinary humanness and frailties of their leaders. When someone has obsessive

175

problems with sexuality and then chooses a religious vocation, it becomes very difficult for them to live with the
adulation and idealized expectations of the laypeople with
whom they work. Living with these expectations intensifies
the "reverse obsession" dynamic that I referred to previously.
The more they try to resist their inner compulsions, the more
their obsession grips them. The internal conflict they feel
because of their inner compulsions increases the need for
secrecy upon which their addiction thrives. Carnes states:

> When the authority of the church was invoked to curtail
> childhood sexual behavior, it provided the essential ingredient
> to psychological obsession: the forbidden. When a child is told
> at the age of five that he will go to hell if he touches his
> genitals, a deep impression is left. Something intensely plea-
> surable is fused with intense sexual and religious shame.
> Combine such experiences with sexual misinformation and
> childhood sexual abuse, and the fusion of the erotic with the
> forbidden assist the potent transition from a moral issue to a
> psychological illness.[12]

What could be more "forbidden" than for a pastor to have a
sexual addiction? Thus the very nature of the problem makes
it all the more potent! Remember, addiction thrives on
secrecy and shame. How many people in a religious vocation
do you think would feel able to share their hidden addiction
with colleagues and people they work with? Yet it is only
when the principles of a Twelve Step recovery program
mediate the healing power of God to an addict that he can
break free of such an addiction. The first step involves
surrender. Admitting our powerlessness over the addiction
and asking God to restore sanity to our life. Addictions thrive
on secrecy and another important component of the Twelve
Steps involves breaking the bond of shame and secrecy by
confession (admitting) to God, oneself, and another human
being the nature of our wrongs (see The Twelve Steps in
Appendix E).

(2) **Guardians of Morality:** This hazard involves the role that clergy must take as leaders in the community. They are expected to be spokespersons for moral issues and values. Pastors are expected to be leaders by example as well as by precept. Thus, they are asked to participate in anti-pornography campaigns as well as other moral crusades. Their vocation requires that they interpret and implement moral authority. Those prone to obsessive disorders will find that their disorder is intensified by these requirements of a religious vocation.[13]

We have recently witnessed in the national media the vilification of certain religious leaders who took very strong public stands against immorality and then who "fell from grace" as the result of certain indiscretions.

(3) **Being in a Trusted Position:** This hazard involves the privileged status of pastors and religious leaders as trusted confidants. Their position of trust gives them authority and power. For a person who is sexually obsessed, this trust allows him to keep his indiscreet behaviors hidden from view. Also, their role as counselors provides pastors an opportunity to become enmeshed in dependency relationships with people who would be most vulnerable to exploitation.

(4) **Emotional Burnout:** This occupational hazard is part of the tendency of pastoral workers to overextend themselves in their service to others. They overextend themselves and become emotionally depleted. Many pastors work alone, or with minimal support staff. The demands on them are rigorous, so they are apt to become overworked. It isn't easy for pastors to avoid being "indispensable" helpers. This can fuel a Messiah-complex mentality. If a pastoral worker believes that they are indispensable and must compulsively minister to others, they foster the type of denial and compulsivity which is necessary to maintain addictive behaviors. Ironically, addicted clergy are sometimes able to help others

177

to face their problems, but they can't see their own situation objectively.

(5) **The Calling:** Some people are attracted to religious vocations as an unconscious means by which they can avoid the conflict produced by sexual addictions and compulsions. It's almost as if they are saying to themselves: "I feel so bad, or am so bad, that I'm going to make up for it by sacrificing my life and committing it to the Lord's work." Actually, the choice of Christian vocation as a cover for shame only makes the problem worse. The veneer of professional uprightness is never thick enough to heal their inner shame. It just conceals it.

Thus, therapists are finding more and more devoutly religious people, including clergy, to be vulnerable to sexual addiction, precisely because of the conditions mentioned above that their religiosity creates. I'm not suggesting that religion causes a person to be sexually addicted. Rather, the religious role creates an environment where sexual addiction can flourish, due to the unresolved secrecy and shame that are part of the addiction cycle for these people. It is simply unacceptable in our culture for pastors and religious leaders to be as fallible as other human beings and struggle with these problems. As a consequence they are isolated, alone, and carry their burden in secret instead of seeking the healing they need. Sexuality is a big secret in the church. We need to bravely confront these issues in our churches so that we can change the atmosphere of secrecy and shame around a topic that promotes the cycle of addiction.

Food is another hidden, and condoned, addiction in the church. Somehow gluttony is overlooked when certain people read the Bible looking for sins against which to rant and rave! Yet under the veneer of their "Sunday best" behavior (and clothes!) lies the horror and pain of eating disorders. Anorexia is rampant as is bulimia. Anorexia is the disorder where a person is afraid of food and systematically stops eating because he is afraid of being "fat." He imagines that he *is* fat when in actuality he is starving, so he uses laxatives, diet pills, and over-exercising to control his weight. Bulimia is the disorder where a person is also afraid of being "fat," though he is usually normal or above average weight, and is compelled to regulate his weight by vomiting after eating. Usually bulimics will gorge themselves with their "forbidden" foods prior to vomiting. Some anorexics end up becoming bulimic as an additional way of managing their weight.

Another common eating disorder is binge-eating. These people do not usually over-exercise or use laxatives, though they may once in a while. Rather, they go in cycles of acting out (binges) and acting in (trying to eat "normally" or "dieting"). They do not purge (vomit) after eating and generally are somewhat overweight, though not always very severely. They are just as obsessed with weight as the anorexic or bulimic. Again, shame feeds their addiction. The more shame they feel, the more they act out; the more they act out, the more shame they feel. Of course, as with any addiction, the people around them become hooked into their cycle, and good, caring codependent Christians offer lots of useless "help." Pastors, Sunday school teachers, elders, or friends get hooked into helping. The same modalities are used as in the previous example with alcoholism: defining the problem spiritually ("She has a demon of gluttony"); defining it psychologically ("He's just depressed so he eats more than other people"); and trying to control it ("Tell your wife she cannot sunbathe [her favorite way to relax] until she loses thirty pounds"—pastor to husband).

This pattern of codependency and enabling can occur elsewhere in the Christian community, too. In a local Christian organization, the boss, a former minister, was clearly a sexual addict. Secretaries and other employees ignored the sexual innuendoes, the coarse jokes, the lewd remarks. When his marriage broke up over another woman, no one blinked twice. Rumors abounded about affairs with various women, including a fellow staff member. Everyone

179

ignored the fact that he maintained a private bedroom on the premises, which was kept locked most of the time! Everyone went along assuming that "nothing was going on" when in reality a lot was going on! Although a number of people have been hurt through this situation being ignored, the consequences have yet to reach a proportion where he has received help. (The one person who tried to confront him was soon thereafter terminated.)

CHRISTIAN LEADERS AS ENABLERS

How do Christian leaders inadvertently enable others to stay stuck in codependency? From my experience there are at least three main ways:

(1) **By not recognizing their own addictive behaviors and/or codependency.** One of the functions of leaders is modeling. If an organization grows or deteriorates from the top down, then what the leaders do is very important. If the pastor or head of the elder board is in denial, others will be too! This denial can have dramatic *or* subtle effects. I knew a pastor at one time who, though an ACA (Adult Child of an Alcoholic) and a workaholic, had never examined his own codependency very deeply. When recovering people came to his church, they felt uncomfortable because he tended to spiritualize addictive behavior and saw recovery as "just trusting Jesus." He had little use for AA or Al Anon or ACA meetings because he did not see the need for them personally. He claimed to have seen someone "who had attended AA for eight years, miraculously healed" upon conversion, so he believed that no one else who was "truly converted" would need AA either!

(2) **By not modeling and teaching the difference between healthy faith and addictive faith.** Many Christian leaders inadvertently drive recovering people away from church! One person recently told me that she changed denominations because she was "tired of being made to feel guilty" that she

did not want to be in church three to five times a week. This lady, a recovering codependent, is the type that when the pastor (or anyone else) said "Jump!" she asked, "How high?" After a while, she saw that her "service" was not out of obedience, or even a true calling from God, but out of a need to "people-please." Yet she remained vulnerable to the pressure directed at her from the pulpit. She said that the "last straw" came on the Sunday morning when the pastor announced that unless people were willing to sign a form promising to be in church twice on Sunday plus Wednesday evening, they could not teach Sunday school! My client handed in her resignation that morning!

(3) **By not educating the Christian community on alcoholism, sexual addiction, eating disorders, workaholism, and codependency, and by not confronting it in their own organizational life.** Codependency and other addictions are rampant in the church, but rarely do you find someone willing to confront them. For example, the case study of Martha at the beginning of this chapter: her pastor has been informed of her codependent behavior by her children and her husband, yet he has yet to confront her.

In another situation, a young woman was hired by a church. Bright and enterprising, this young woman charmed her way into the hearts of all who met her. However, her charm had a darker side: It enabled her to be a proficient liar! When this problem was uncovered, it was assumed to be a spiritual issue and a spiritual solution was prescribed: She was farmed out to live with one of the church leadership. The assumption was that if she were properly "discipled" and loved, the problem would rectify itself. Unfortunately, it did not and the lying continued unabated for a number of years. Later on in therapy, after a failed marriage, she realized that she was deeply addicted to caretaking and had been sexually victimized as a child. No one in her home church or in the church which employed her had realized she was a codependent, or that by spiritualizing the problem, they were not being helpful.

MAJORING IN THE MINORS

The other day a pastor's wife told me of her frustration with their new church. A church of some five hundred people, it is in that awkward stage between a large church and a medium-sized church. There are three full-time staff people and a part-time Christian education person. Located in the center of a busy metropolitan area, it has lots of potential for growth, and a big need for organization, new goals, structure, and guidance. The pastor's wife has wanted to throw her intelligence and energy into some of the areas of need within the church but has found people focused on petty things instead. Typical of the issues that consume the church people are: anger at the head pastor for stepping "out of the pulpit" while holding the Bible as he was preaching one Sunday morning and strife over the need for Women's Bible Studies (there were none in the church) because it might "compete" with the Ladies Aid Society.

Are we being wise stewards of the gospel? Are we creating the kind of atmosphere that helps people grow? I do not think so. Rare is the church where people feel free to be honest, where people dare say what they really feel, where women and men can own up to struggles and fear without worrying about looking less spiritual. We have failed dismally. What can we do?

THE CHURCH AS A THERAPEUTIC COMMUNITY

Dr. Gary Sweeten, director of LIFE Seminars (see Appendix D), formerly the Christian Discipleship pastor at College Hill Presbyterian Church in Cincinnati, has worked for the last twenty years to find an answer to this problem. Dr. Sweeten did his doctoral dissertation on equipping laypeople in the local church with the goal of creating a "therapeutic community" where "substantial healing" could occur.[14]

Four years later, under his leadership, I completed my own dissertation in the same area, extending the process further. For a number of years now Dr. Sweeten and I and many others have worked together to spread the vision of a therapeutic community. The LIFE Seminars are Dr. Sweeten's latest brainchild to equip church leaders outside our local area in the skills necessary to create a therapeutic community. Over the last fifteen years, thousands of pastors and laypeople have been equipped all over the world by Dr. Sweeten and his team. He has traveled across the United States, to Europe and to South Africa to spread "the word." Leaders of the evangelical movement in Scandinavia have recently told him that the principles taught in the LIFE seminar will be the key to the reevangelization of Europe in the next twenty years. YWAM (Youth with a Mission) recently adopted his training materials for all their counseling centers worldwide!

What does a "therapeutic community" look like? A therapeutic community is above all else a "safe place"—a place where broken people can come and struggle together without condemnation. It is a place where no matter what clothes they wear, or how much their automobile costs, they are given love and respect as a fellow human being. A therapeutic community is a place where laypeople and clergy are trained to listen and help one another and to pray and invoke God's supernatural power in everyday life; where people expect God to keep His promises. It is a place where people are congruent (what you see is what you get) and genuineness pervades the atmosphere. There is no competition to look most spiritual or a fear of honest self-disclosure. Confrontation is done in love, with a foundation of sincere empathy and respect. Concerns are dealt with in the here and now, rather than being stored up for weeks, months, or years. There is a sense of honest immediacy in a place where people are building a therapeutic community.

It is a place where everyone understands that "the ground at the Cross is level" as John Sandford always says, where no one needs to be defensive because we are all in the same boat! It is a place where a struggler can find support in weakness, freedom to fail and try again, and accountability as he goes along.

It is beyond the scope of this book to explain how to create a therapeutic community. Dr. Sweeten does that very well in the LIFE Seminars. (See Appendix D.) Suffice it to say, although no church will ever become a *perfect* therapeutic community, substantial growth and healing in relationships and in community life can occur. Indeed it has occurred, all over the world, wherever people have been willing to be open to new ideas and to stop majoring in minors.

If we are to become the stewards of Christ's love and power in our world today, which the Scripture calls us to be; if our churches are to become "Safe Places" for codependent people to come, where addicted people can find help and healing, where sexually abused children can find healthy role models, then we must wake up and begin to change our structures, our plans, our visions, our goals. Codependency, addiction, and abuse are not going to go away. Today even small towns out in the country are being invaded by drugs. Sexual addiction is becoming more common. Evangelical pastors and Roman Catholic priests are being accused of child molestation. Divorce is tearing at the fabric of Christian homes, even ministers' homes. These problems are not going to become less in the next twenty years. They will get worse and increase exponentially. We must act now!

9

ONE WOMAN'S STORY

Faced with codependency—your own or someone else's, faced with an addiction—yours or a loved one's, what can you do? You may feel you cannot do anything, that you are too weak or broken yourself for God to use you. The reality is, however, that God *can* heal you and use you if you are open. The story of a friend of mine is proof that all it takes to be healed and used is openness to God's Spirit. My friend, whom I will call Paula, is the wife of a well-known church leader. Her husband is involved in a number of internationally recognized ministries. Over the years, Paula has been a quiet support to her husband, running their home efficiently and caring for their children. Most people in their church knew her only as an attractive, quiet person who loved being a homemaker until three years ago! Three years ago Paula experienced a new touch of God in her life. All of her life she had carried a secret burden about which few people knew. In fact, she had tried to ignore it herself. The reality was that Paula came from an alcoholic family. Having become a Christian in college when a friend shared Christ with her, Paula had for years tried to make sense of the inner pain, depression, and guilt that she carried around with her. She

was sure it was because she was not "good enough" as a
Christian or because of some fundamental flaw within herself.
As the wife of a Christian leader, she thought she needed to
look perfect so she never let on to anyone how she was
feeling. Reading books, going to seminars, praying harder
never seemed to make much difference. She tried over and
over to solve the problem alone. After a while Paula decided
that the victorious, happy, fulfilled Christian life was for other
people, and that for herself, she would just hang in there and
wait for heaven or the Second Coming!

One day a friend gave her some information on Adult
Children of Alcoholics. At first, though she found it interesting, Paula did not grasp the full impact of the material for her
life. Meanwhile, God was convicting her to speak to two
prayer warriors, Sam and Denise, who ministered to people
through prayer and listening at their church. She resisted a
long while but finally went. Over the next few months, Paula
poured out her heart to them about her pain, rage, and
confusion, especially over the alcoholism in her family.
Praying with her, struggling alongside her, laughing and
crying with her, Sam and Denise modeled true compassion
and nonjudgmental acceptance to Paula. For the first time,
she began to feel free—free to be herself—free to drop the
perfectionistic fasade, free to explore the effects of her
codependency on her marriage and her relationship to her
children.

Discovering her codependent patterns was just the beginning point for Paula. Reviewing her past history with her
family of origin and examining present relationships was very
painful. She began to realize how important forgiveness is
and that while she was not responsible for her parents'
alcoholism. She was now as an adult, responsible for her
continuing response to it. One of the biggest discoveries that
she made was that she did have choices—she was not a
powerless victim who could only live in reaction to others.
Paula began to see change, very slowly, in the way she

186

interacted with her family and friends. Like other recovering people, she found that life was full of "one step forward—two steps back" experiences. Even today, she is careful to point out that she has not "arrived" and that she still is "becoming" whole.

I can still remember the Sunday Paula gave her testimony in a special church service. Many people had never heard her speak previously, since she had usually kept in the background. As she spoke, a hush fell over the packed auditorium. Tears were shed, and when she finished, the place erupted with applause. For many people, having someone who looked so together stand up and talk openly about her problems, fears, anger, and pain was a total revelation! The next few weeks saw the local Christian counseling center flooded with calls from Christians who were also Adult Children of Alcoholics. Paula's courage had given them courage to face their own pain and to seek help.

Since then, Paula has made a number of trips, overseas and here in the States, to share her testimony and to pray for others as part of a healing team. Paula has started a dozen "Step Groups" for Christian Adult Children of Alcoholics and has discipled others to lead the groups. Over the last two years, she has also founded a Christian ACA Support Group. All of this, because of the courage of one woman to face her pain and let God work through her.

You may be overwhelmed with pain or guilt or fear after reading this book and having confronted your own neediness for the first time. Take heart! Paula's life is a shining testimony to God's healing power, and God is as much available to you as to her! Dealing with codependency takes courage, but you can do it! You are not alone! God bless you as you take those first steps! God can use you!

APPENDIX A—
"MY RECOVERY PLAN"

Name: _____ Therapist: _____

Date: _____ Sponsor: _____

My Personal Recovery Goals

1 month _____

3 months _____

6 months _____

5 years _____

My Support System

Sponsor _____

Support groups _____

Friends who understand recovery _____

Family members who understand recovery _____

Church/pastoral support _____

Other _____

My Relapse Prevention Guide

Situations where I am vulnerable to relapse (e.g., family reunions, holidays, birthdays, going with Sam in his car, when kids are away visiting their father):

What I will do to avoid these situations or minimize their impact: _____

_____

_____

_____

People who have a negative effect on my recovery: _____

_____

_____

_____

What I will do to avoid these people or minimize their effect on me: _____

_____

_____

_____

My signs of burnout (e.g., losing my car keys, bouncing checks, swearing, losing weight, losing my time card, forgetting to water my plants, missing a meeting): _____

_____

_____

_____

What I will do when I notice three or more of these burnout signals at one time in my life: _____

_____

_____

_____

My plan to handle relapses, if they happen.

1. I will contact _____

2. Spiritually I will _____

3. Emotionally I will _____

4. To handle shame I will _____

5. To handle guilt I will _____

6. To get back into recovery I will _____

Signed: _____

Date: _____

APPENDIX B—
COUNSELING RESOURCES

Several of the following organizations maintain directories of Christian psychologists and other mental health professionals in various geographical areas of the country. These organizations may be able to refer you to other qualified organizations and individual practitioners in your own community.

Focus On The Family (Dr. James Dobson)
Counseling Department
801 Corporate Center Drive
Pomona, California 91768
1-714-620-8500

Has a nationally syndicated radio program and publishes a monthly magazine.

Minirith-Meier Clinic
2100 North Collins Boulevard
Richardson, Texas 75080
1-800-232-9462

Provides a national network of Christ-centered health-care facilities staffed by Christian professionals; specializes in psychiatric, psychological, and substance-abuse treatment; and has an excellent nationally syndicated, daily radio program about psychological issues from a Christian perspective.

Rapha
8876 Gulf Freeway, Suite 130
Houston, Texas 77017
1-800-227-2657

Provides a national network of quality Christ-centered health care by credentialed health-care providers and specializes in psychiatric and substance abuse treatment.

The Christian Information Committee
LIFE Seminars
P.O. Box 24080
Cincinnati, Ohio 45224
1-513-541-7500

Life Seminars offers equipping and training courses in interpersonal skills for lay leaders and clergy and a consistent schedule of training seminars with training materials available in printed, audio, and video tape format.

APPENDIX C—
RESOURCE READING LIST

The following references may be helpful to readers who desire further information on the topic of codependency. Dr. Rinck does not necessarily agree with or endorse all viewpoints espoused by these authors. Not all authors listed here represent a Christian evangelical worldview in their discussion of codependency and related topics; however, their works present useful information about codependency and can be profitably read by the discerning reader.

Inner Healing and Spiritual Development

Foster, Richard. *Celebration of Discipline: The Path to Spiritual Growth.* San Francisco: Harper & Row, 1978.

Kiersey, David and Bates, Marilyn. *Please Understand Me.* Del Mar: California: Prometheus Nemesis Books, 1978.

Linn, Matthew and Dennis. *Healing Life's Hurts.* New York: Paulist, 1978.

Payne, Leanne. *The Broken Image: Restoring Personal Wholeness Through Healing Prayer.* Westchester, Illinois: Crossway, 1981.

Payne, Leanne. *Crisis in Masculinity.* Westchester, Illinois: Crossway, 1985.

Rubin, Theodore Isaac. *The Angry Book.* New York: Macmillan, 1969.

Sandford, J. A. *Dreams and Healing.* New York: Paulist, 1978. Bl Sandford, John and Paula. *Transformation of the Inner Man.* S. Plainfield, New Jersey: Bridge Publishing Company, 1982.

Smedes, Lewis B. *Forgive and Forget: Healing the Hurts That We Don't Deserve.* New York: Pocket Books, 1984.

Can Christians Love Too Much?

Male and Female Relationships

Beattie, Melody. *Codependent No More.* Center City, Minnesota: Hazelden Educational Materials, 1987.

Bessell, Howard. *The Love Test.* New York: Wm. Morrow and Company, 1984.

Black, Claudia. *It'll Never Happen To Me.* Denver: M.A.C. Printing and Publications, 1981.

Carnes, Patrick. *Out Of the Shadows.* Minneapolis: Comp Care, 1983.

Carter, Steven. *Men Who Can't Love.* New York: M. Evans & Company, 1987.

Cowan, Connell and Kinder, Melvyn. *Smart Women: Foolish Choices.* New York: Clarkson and Potter, Inc., 1985.

Cruise, Sharon W. *Choice-Making.* Pompano Beach, Florida: Health Communications, 1985.

Forward, Susan. *Men Who Hate Women and the Women Who Love Them.* New York: Bantam Books, 1986.

Kiley, Dan. *The Peter Pan Syndrome.* New York: Avon Books, 1983.

Kiley, Dan. *The Wendy Dilemma.* New York: Arbor House, 1984.

Leonard, Linda Schierse. *The Wounded Woman: Healing the Father-Daughter Relationship.* Boston: Shambula, 1982.

Sanford, J. A. *Invisible Partners.* New York: Paulist, 1980.

Shainess, Natalie. *Sweet Suffering: Woman as Victim.* Indianapolis: Bobbs-Merrill Co., Inc., 1984.

Strom, Kay Marshall. *In the Name of Submission: A Painful Look at Wife-Battering.* Portland, Oregon: Multnomah Press, 1986.

Codependency and Recovery

Larsen, Earnie. *Stage II Relationships: Love Beyond Addiction.* San Francisco: Harper & Row, 1987.

Lenters, William. *The Freedom We Crave: Addiction—The Human Condition.* Grand Rapids: Eerdmans, 1985.

Middleton-Moz, Jane and Dwinell, Lorie. *After the Tears: Reclaiming the Personal Losses of Childhood.* Pompano Beach, Florida: Health Communications, 1986.

Rinck, Margaret J. *When Love Hurts: Codependency and Interpersonal Relationships.* Cincinnati: Act Resources, 1988.

Schneider, Jennifer P. *Back from Betrayal: Recovering from His Affairs.* Center City, Minnesota: Hazelden Educational Materials, 1988.

Schaef, Anne Wilson. *Codependence: Misunderstood—Mistreated.* San Francisco: Harper & Row, 1986.

Woititz, Janet. *Adult Children of Alcoholics.* Hollywood, Florida: Health Communications, 1983.

Appendix C—Resource Reading List

Woititz, Janet. *Home Away from Home: The Art of Self-Sabotage.* Pompano Beach, Florida: Health Communications, 1987.

Woititz, Janet. *Struggle for Intimacy.* Pompano Beach, Florida: Health Communications, 1985.

Workbooks

Black, Claudia. *Repeat After Me.* Denver: M.A.C. Printing and Publishing, 1985.

Carnes, Patrick. *A Gentle Way Through the 12 Steps.* CompCare Publications, 1989.

God Help Me Stop. Anonymous. (P.O. Box 27364, San Diego, CA 92128).

The Twelve Steps: A Spiritual Journey (Anon. Recovery Publications). 1201 Knoxville Street, San Diego, CA 92110).

Books to Help You Cope

Brilles, Judith. *Dollars and Sense of Divorce.* New York: Master Media Ltd., 1988.

Brilles, Judith. *Faith and Savvy Too.* New York: Master Media Ltd., 1988.

Brilles, Judith. *Woman to Woman: From Sabotage to Support.* Far Hills, New Jersey, 1987.

Drews, Toby Rice. *Getting Them Sober* (Vols. 1–3), S. Plainfield, New Jersey: Bridge Publishing, 1980, 1983, 1986.

Hart, Archibald. *Adrenalin and Stress.* Waco, Texas: Word, 1986.

APPENDIX D—LIFE SEMINARS

In chapter 8, I referenced the importance of the church as a therapeutic community. LIFE Seminars/Christian Information Committee, Inc. is one of the few organizations of which I am aware that fundamentally integrates the Christian worldview with psychology and educational resources to provide a systematic training program to church leaders for renewal in the local church. Renewal in the local church is a key issue for the Christian community as we attempt to address institutional issues of codependency in our midst.

In addition to their catalog of workshops and programs in book, audio cassette, and video tape cassette form, LIFE Seminars (Leadership in Foundational Equipping) offers regular training workshops.

Goal: To help pastors and other church leaders to be successful in ministry.

Objective: To make the church of Jesus Christ into a caring, healing, growth community.

Means: To enable pastors and other leaders to effectively and practically know how to "equip their members so that they are actually doing the work of ministry."

Workshops and available materials include:

Apples of Gold I—Developing the Fruit of the Spirit: How to develop interpersonal skills training for empathy, warmth, and respect in relationships (a foundational course).

Apples of Gold II—Speaking the Truth in Love: How to confront in love; resist inappropriate behavior; deal with angry people; manage conflict; and move others to positive action steps.

Rational Christian Thinking—Renewing the Mind: How to deal with anxiety-provoking thoughts, depression, compulsions, and fears, including the importance of mind in Scripture, how to train yourself to think rationally, and how to combat irrational self-talk.

Breaking Free from the Past—Healing Life's Hurts: How to focus on mutual confession, forgiveness, and intercessory prayer (recommended for mature, well-trained people with caring and self-awareness skills; requires as prerequisite all of the above listed courses plus other requirements).

The Theology of a Caring, Equipping Community: How to integrate psychology, theology, and the power of the Holy Spirit and practical considerations for setting up a lay counseling center.

Growing As a Christian Family: How to aid the family and the church congregation in becoming places of healing and growth (a pilot workshop developed by a family therapist).

Won By One—Friendship Evangelism: How to effectively help friends and family (including children) discover a personal relationship with Jesus Christ (based on Dr. Ronald Rand's book of the same title).

Small Groups—Workable Wineskins: How to handle many aspects of small group life, focusing upon ways groups can be used in the church; communicating effectively to build relationships; stages groups go through; various other group dynamics and some practical how-to's for the functioning and growth of groups.

Training Lay Pastors: How to provide pastoral care for every member of the church body by calling forth and equipping laypeople who have pastoral gifts.

In addition to the above courses, other courses are available to train participants to teach the foundational courses in their own local congregations.

For more information about training and courses, write to

Christian Information Committee, Inc.
LIFE Seminars
P.O. Box 24080
Cincinnati, Ohio 45224
(513) 541-7500

APPENDIX E—THE TWELVE STEPS

Step One

We admitted that we were powerless over our separation from God—that our lives had become unmanageable.

I know that nothing good lives in me, that is, in my sinful nature. For I have the desire to do what is good, but I cannot carry it out (Romans 7:18).

Step Two

We came to believe that a power greater than ourselves could restore us to sanity.

For it is God who works in you to will and to act according to his good purpose (Philippians 2:13).

Step Three

We made a decision to turn our will and our lives over to the care of God as we understood Him.

Therefore, I urge you, brothers, in view of God's mercy, to offer your bodies as living sacrifices, holy and pleasing to God—this is your spiritual act of worship (Romans 12:1).

Step Four

We made a searching and fearless moral inventory of ourselves.

Let us examine our ways and test them, and let us return to the LORD (Lamentations 3:40).

Step Five

We admitted to God, to ourselves, and to another human being the exact nature of our wrongs.

Therefore confess your sins to each other and pray for each other so that you may be healed (James 5:16a).

Step Six

We were entirely ready to have God remove all these defects of character.

Humble yourselves before the Lord, and he will lift you up (James 4:10).

Step Seven

We humbly asked Him to remove our shortcomings.

If we confess our sins, he is faithful and just and will forgive us our sins and purify us from all unrighteousness (1 John 1:9).

Step Eight

We made a list of all persons we had harmed and became willing to make amends to them all.

Do to others as you would have them do to you (Luke 6:31).

Step Nine

We made direct amends to such people wherever possible, except when to do so would injure them or others.

Therefore, if you are offering your gift at the altar and there remember that your brother has something against you, leave your gift there in front of the altar. First go and be reconciled to your brother; then come and offer your gift (Matthew 5:23–24).

Step Ten

We continued to take personal inventory, and when we were wrong, promptly admitted it.

So, if you think you are standing firm, be careful that you don't fall (1 Corinthians 10:12).

Step Eleven

We sought through prayer and meditation to improve our conscious contact with God as we understood Him, praying only for knowledge of His will for us and the power to carry that out.

Let the word of Christ dwell in you richly (Colossians 3:16a).

Step Twelve

Having had a spiritual awakening as the result of these steps, we tried to carry this message to others, and to practice these principles in our affairs.

Brothers, if someone is caught in a sin, you who are spiritual should restore him gently. But watch yourself, or you also may be tempted (Galatians 6:1).

From The Twelve Steps—A Spiritual Journey, pp. xiii–xiv.

NOTES

Chapter 1

[1]Lewis, C. S., *The Great Divorce* (New York: The Macmillan Company, 1946), 93.

Chapter 2

[1]Norwood, Robin, *Women Who Love Too Much* (Los Angeles: Jeremy P. Tarcher, Inc., 1986), passim.

[2]Schaef, Anne Wilson, *Codependence: Misunderstood—Mistreated* (San Francisco: Harper and Row Publishers, 1986), 5.

[3]Ibid., 6.

[4]Black, Claudia, *It'll Never Happen To Me* (Denver: M.A.C. Printing and Publications, 1981), passim.

[5]Woititz, Janet G., *Struggle for Intimacy* (Pompano Beach, Florida: Health Communications, 1985), passim.

[6]Schaef, Anne Wilson, *Codependence: Misunderstood—Mistreated*, 6.

[7]Friel, John and Linda, *Adult Children* (Deerfield Beach, Florida: Health Communication, Inc., 1988), 157.

[8]Beattie, Melody, *Codependent No More* (Center City, Minnesota: Hazelden, 1987), 85–86.

[9]Sandford, Linda T. and Donovan, Mary Ellen, *Women and Self-Esteem* (New York: Penguin Books, 1984), 168.

[10]May, Gerald, *Grace and Addiction* (San Francisco: Harper and Row, Inc., 1988), 37.

[11]Wegscheider-Cruse, Sharon, *Choice-Making* (Pompano Beach, Florida: Health Communications, 1985), 2.

12 Schaeffer, Brenda, *Is It Love or Is It Addiction?* (Center City, Minnesota: Hazelden Educational Materials, 1988), 5.

13 Subby, Robert, "Inside the Chemically Dependent Marriage: Denial and Manipulation," *Codependency, An Emerging Issue* (Pompano Beach, Florida.: Health Communications, 1984): 26.

14 Cermak, Timmen L., M.D., *Diagnosing and Treating Co-Dependence* (Minneapolis: Johnson Institute, 1986), 32–33.

Chapter 3

1 Schaeffer, *Is It Love or Is It Addiction?*, passim.; Norwood, *Women Who Love Too Much*, passim.

2 Lenters, William, *The Freedom We Crave: Addiction—The Human Condition* (Grand Rapids: Wm. Eerdmans Co., 1985), 88.

3 Schaeffer, *Is It Love or Is It Addiction?*, 38–59.

Chapter 4

1 Nobel, Lowell L., *Naked and Not Ashamed* (Jackson, Michigan: Jackson Printing, 1975), 20–23.

2 Ibid.

3 Benedict, Ruth, *The Chrysanthemum and the Sword* (Boston: Houghton-Mifflin, 1946), passim.

4 Lynd, Helen Merrell, *On Shame and the Search for Identity* (Eugene, Oregon: Harvest House Publications, 1958), 19–20.

5 Nobel, *Naked and Not Ashamed*, 2–3.

6 Ibid., 5.

7 Ibid., 4–5.

8 Bradshaw, John, *Healing the Shame That Binds You* (Deerfield Beach, Florida: Health Communications, 1988), 88.

9 Ibid., 52–53.

10 Ibid., 41–44.

11 Ibid., 46.

12 Mouw, Richard, "The Life of Bondage in the Light of Grace," *Christianity Today* 32 (December 9, 1988): 41–44.

13 Bradshaw, *Healing the Shame That Binds You*, 56.

14 Bloom-Feshbach, Jonathan and Sally, *The Psychology of Separation and Loss* (San Francisco: Jossey-Bass Publishers, 1987), passim.

15 Ibid., 109–135.

16 Ibid., 29.

17 Bowlby, J., *Attachment and Loss* (New York: Basic Books, 1969, 1973, 1980), passim.

Notes

[18]Joy, Donald, *Bonding* (Waco, Texas: Word Publications, 1985), passim.
[19]Joy, Donald, *Re-Bonding* (Waco, Texas: Word Publications, 1986), passim.

Chapter 5

[1]Rinck, Margaret Josephson, *Renewing Your Mind* (Fairfield, Ohio: Lay Leadership International, 1984), 1–4.
[2]Nobel, *Naked and Not Ashamed*, 5.
[3]Ibid., 3.
[4]Carnes, Patrick, *Counseling the Sexual Addict*, Symposium presented at the Institute of Behavioral Medicine, Golden Valley, Minnesota (September 1988), passim.
[5]Hart, Archibald D., "Addicted to Pleasure," *Christianity Today* 32 (December 9, 1988): 39–40.
[6]Cohen, Sidney, *The Chemical Brain: The Neurochemistry of Addictive Disease* (Minneapolis: Care Institute, 1988), passim.
[7]Fitzgerald, Kathleen Whalen, Ph.D., *Alcoholism: The Genetic Inheritance* (New York: Doubleday, 1988), passim.
[8]Hart, "Addicted to Pleasure," 39–40.
[9]Lenters, *The Freedom We Crave: Addiction—The Human Condition*, 69.
[10]Mouw, "The Life of Bondage in the Light of Grace," 41.
[11]Lenters, *The Freedom We Crave: Addiction—The Human Condition*, 70.
[12]Mouw, "The Life of Bondage in the Light of Grace," 42.
[13]Sweeten, Gary Ray, *Breaking Free From the Past* (Cincinnati, Ohio: Christian Information Committee, 1983), 1–7, 11–13.
[14]Alsdurf, Jim and Phyllis, "The Generic Disease," *Christianity Today* 32 (December 9, 1988): 37–38.

Chapter 6

[1]Black, *It'll Never Happen To Me*, 13–104.
[2]Woititz, *Struggle for Intimacy*, passim.
[3]Wegscheider-Cruse, *Choice-Making*, 163–168.
[4]Sloat, Donald E., *The Dangers of Growing Up in a Christian Home* (New York: Thomas Nelson Publishers, 1986), passim.
[5]Woititz, *Struggle for Intimacy*, 13–18.
[6]Rentzel, Lori Thorkelson, *Emotional Dependency: A Threat to Close Friendships* (San Rafael, California: Exodus International, 1984), 7.
[7]Ibid., 8.
[8]Ibid., 8–9.

Can Christians Love Too Much?

Chapter 7

[1] Friends in Recovery, *The Twelve Steps—A Spiritual Journey* (San Diego: Recovery Publications, 1988), ix.

[2] Ibid., xii.

[3] Carnes, *Counseling the Sexual Addict*, passim.

[4] Buie, James, "Twelve Step Program Can Boast Therapy" *The APA Monitor* 18 (November 1987): 12.

[5] A sponsor is a person who has been in a Twelve Step recovery program for at least one year and has made substantial progress in his own personal recovery. Sponsors often provide emotional support, will challenge, and provide accountability and guidance to assist a person in Twelve Step recovery.

[6] Carnes, *Counseling the Sexual Addict*, passim.

[7] Ibid.

[8] Norwood, *Women Who Love Too Much*, 57.

[9] Maultsby, Maxie C., Jr., *Help Yourself to Happiness Through Rational Self-Counseling* (New York: Institute for Rational Living, Inc., 1975), 7–52.

[10] Rinck, Margaret Josephson, *Christian Men Who Hate Women* (Cincinnati: Act Resources, P.O. Box 24177, Cincinnati, Ohio 45224, 1988), passim.

[11] Sloat, *The Dangers of Growing Up in a Christian Home*, 147.

[12] Ibid., 147, 150.

[13] Foster, Richard J., *Celebration of Discipline: The Path to Spiritual Growth* (San Francisco: Harper and Row Publishers, 1978), 112-113.

[14] Klagsburn, Francine, *Married People: Staying Together in an Age of Divorce* (New York: Bantam Books, 1989), 23.

[15] Carter, Steven and Sokal, Julia, *Men Who Can't Love* (New York: Berkley Books, 1975), passim.

[16] Rinck, Margaret Josephson, *Male-Female Relationships: Discovering Unhealthy Patterns* (Cincinnati: Act Resources, P.O. Box 24177, Cincinnati, Ohio 45224, 1988), passim.

[17] Harley, Willard, *His Needs, Her Needs: Building an Affair-Proof Marriage* (Old Tappan: Fleming H. Revell Company, 1986), 72–86.

Chapter 8

[1] Schaef, Anne Wilson and Diane Fassel, *The Addictive Organization* (San Francisco: Harper and Row Publishers, 1988), 119–122.

[2] Ibid., 119–122.

[3] Ibid., 123.

[4] Ibid., 122–125.

[5] Ibid., 123–124.

Notes

[6] Lenters, *The Freedom We Crave: Addiction—The Human Condition*, 82.

[7] Ibid., 92.

[8] Schaef and Fassel, *The Addictive Organization*, 80.

[9] Ibid., 90–91.

[10] Carnes, *Counseling the Sexual Addict*, passim.

[11] Carnes, Patrick, "Sexual Addiction: Implications for Spiritual Formation," *Journal of On-Going Formation* VII (May 1987): 169.; *Counseling the Sexual Addict*, passim.

[12] Carnes, "Sexual Addiction: Implications for Spiritual Formation," 169.

[13] Ibid.

[14] Sweeten, Gary R., *Training of Lay People in the Local Church*, Doctoral Dissertation, University of Cincinnati, Dissertation Abstracts International, 1975, passim.

BIBLIOGRAPHY

Alsdurf, Jim and Phyllis. "The Generic Disease." *Christianity Today* 32 (December 9, 1988): 30–38.

Beattie, Melody. *Codependent No More*. Center City, Minnesota: Hazelden Educational Materials, 1987.

Benedict, Ruth. *The Chrysanthemum and the Sword*. Boston: Houghton-Mifflin, 1946.

Black, Claudia. *It'll Never Happen To Me*. Denver: M.A.C. Printing and Publications, 1981.

Bloom-Feshbach, Jonathan and Sally. *The Psychology of Separation and Loss*. San Francisco: Jossey-Bass Publishers, 1987.

Bowlby, J. *Attachment and Loss* Vol. 1–3, New York: Basic Books, 1969, 1973, 1980.

Bradshaw, John. *Healing the Shame that Binds You*. Deerfield Beach, Florida: Health Communications, 1988.

Buie, James. "12 Step Program Can Boast Therapy." *The APA Monitor* 18 (November, 1987).

Carnes, Patrick. "Sexual Addiction: Implications for Spiritual Formation." *Journal of On-going Formation* VII (May, 1987).

Carnes, Patrick. *Counseling the Sexual Addict*. Symposium presented at the Institute of Behavioral Medicine, Golden Valley, Minnesota (September, 1988).

Carter, Steven and Julia Sokal. *Men Who Can't Love*. New York: Berkley Books, 1975.

Cermak, Timmen L., M.D. *Diagnosing and Treating Co-dependence*. Minneapolis: Johnson Institute, 1986.

Foster, Richard J. *Celebration of Discipline: The Path to Spiritual Growth*. San Francisco: Harper & Row, 1978.

Friel, John and Linda. *Adult Children*. Deerfield Beach, Florida: Health Communications, Inc., 1988.

Can Christians Love Too Much?

Friends in Recovery. *The Twelve Steps—A Spiritual Journey*. San Francisco: Jossey-Bass Publishers, 1987.

Harley, Willard. *His Needs, Her Needs: Building an Affair-Proof Marriage*. Old Tappan: Revell, 1986.

Hart, Archibald D. "Addicted to Pleasure." *Christianity Today* 32 (December 9, 1988): 39–40.

Hatterson, Lawrence. *The Pleasure Addicts*. San Diego: A. S. Barnes and Co., 1980.

Joy, Donald. *Bonding*. Waco, Texas: Word, 1985.

Joy, Donald. *Re-Bonding*. Waco, Texas: Word, 1986.

Klagsburn, Francine. *Married People: Staying Together in an Age of Divorce*. New York: Bantam Books, 1989.

Lenters, William. *The Freedom We Crave: Addiction—The Human Condition*. Grand Rapids: Eerdmans, 1985

Lewis, C. S. *The Great Divorce*. New York: The Macmillan Company, 1946.

Lynd, Helen Merrell. *On Shame and the Search for Identity*. Eugene, Oregon: Harvest House Publications, 1958.

Maultsby, Maxie C., Jr. *Help Yourself to Happiness Through Rational Self-Counseling*. New York: Institute for Rational Living, Inc., 1975.

May, Gerald. *Grace and Addiction*. San Francisco: Harper & Row, 1988.

Mouw, Richard. "The Life of Bondage in the Light of Grace." *Christianity Today* 32 (December 9, 1988): 41–44.

Nobel, Lowell L. *Naked and Not Ashamed*. Jackson: Jackson Printing, 1975.

Norwood, Robin. *Women Who Love Too Much*. Los Angeles: Jeremy P. Tarcher, Inc., 1986.

Rentzel, Lori Thorkelson. *Emotional Dependency: A Threat to Close Friendships*. San Rafael, California: Exodus International, 1984.

Rinck, Margaret J. *Male-Female Relationships: Discovering Unhealthy Patterns*. Cincinnati: Act Resources, 1988.

Rinck, Margaret Josephson, *Renewing Your Mind*. Fairfield, Ohio: Lay Leadership International, 1984.

Rinck, Margaret J., *Christian Men Who Hate Women*. Cincinnati: Act Resources, 1988.

Sandford, Linda T. and Mary Ellen Donovan. *Women and Self-Esteem*. New York: Penguin Books, 1984.

Schaef, Anne Wilson. *Co-dependence: Misunderstood-Mistreated*. San Francisco: Harper & Row, 1986.

Schaeffer, Brenda. *Is It Love or Is It Addiction?*. Center City, Minnesota: Hazelden Educational Materials, 1988.

Sloat, Donald E. *The Dangers of Growing Up in a Christian Home*. New York: Nelson, 1986.

Bibliography

Subby, Robert. "Inside the Chemically Dependent Marriage: Denial and Manipulation." *Co-dependency, An Emerging Issue.* Pompano Beach, Florida: Health Communications, 1984.

Sweeten, Gary R. *Training of Lay People in the Local Church.* Doctoral Dissertation, University of Cincinnati. Dissertation Abstracts International, 1975.

Wegscheider-Cruse, Sharon. *Coupleship: How to Have a Relationship.* Deerfield Beach, Florida: Health Communications, 1988.

Woititz, Janet. *Struggle for Intimacy.* Pompano Beach, Florida: Health Communications, 1985.

RECOMMENDED CASSETTE TAPES

Dr. Rinck's seminars, workshops, and lectures have been professionally recorded and are available on cassette tape. For a brochure and ordering information on these and other tapes, write to

ACT RESOURCES
Audio Counseling Training Resources
P.O. Box 24177, Department Z
Cincinnati, Ohio 45224

Male and Female Relationships: Discovering Unhealthy Patterns—how do past family patterns and relationships affect our present relationships? This ten-cassette series examines the dynamics of interpersonal relationships. Particular emphasis is on the study of four unhealthy patterns that occur in male-female relationships: (1) unequal balance of power—man as controller/woman as victim; (2) immaturity: games in relationships; (3) love as addiction: codependency; and (4) relationship burnout. The first half of the tapes suggests how these patterns may be realigned. Guidelines are included for developing healthy relationships based on emotional maturity.

When Love Hurts: Codependency and Interpersonal Relationships—a four-cassette series that deals comprehensively with the subject of codependency. Dr. Rinck integrates information from a wide spectrum of available codependency literature. Topics include: (1) Definition of codependency: What is codependency? How is it expressed in relationships? Who is vulnerable to the codependency syndrome? (2) Characteristics of codependent relationships: How do I know if I am in a codependent relationship? What are the signs of an addictive relationship? (3) Characteristics of codependent people: What personality and behavioral traits do codependent people exhibit? How is codependency perpetuated in relationships? (4) Freedom from codependency: How do I break the cycle of codependency? How do I understand the spiritual dynamics of codependency?

Christians and Codependency—an extensive eight-cassette tape series on codependency that is a companion to Dr. Rinck's book, *Can Christians Love Too Much?*

Christian Men Who Hate Women—a description of the dynamics of misogynistic relationships. What are the characteristics of abusive relationships? What are the characteristics of the Christian misogynist? What kind of woman marries a misogynist? What background factors produce a misogynistic relationship? What are the issues for the Christian community? This material is from Dr. Rinck's ninety minute workshop on misogyny presented at the International Congress on Christian Counseling (Atlanta '88).

Issues in Psychology and Counseling—a description of the types of issues that people may bring into the counseling setting, presented to a group of paraprofessional counselors at a church counseling center.

Celebration of Marriage: Christian Women and Marriage—a discussion of marital issues and Christian values (one cassette).

Emotions in the Family—a description of family relationships and how to deal with emotions in a positive manner (three cassettes).

Relationship Between Health and Stress—discussion of how stress affects our emotional and physical health, steps we can take to deal with stress in a healthy way (one cassette).